Weeping Mary

2

Welcome

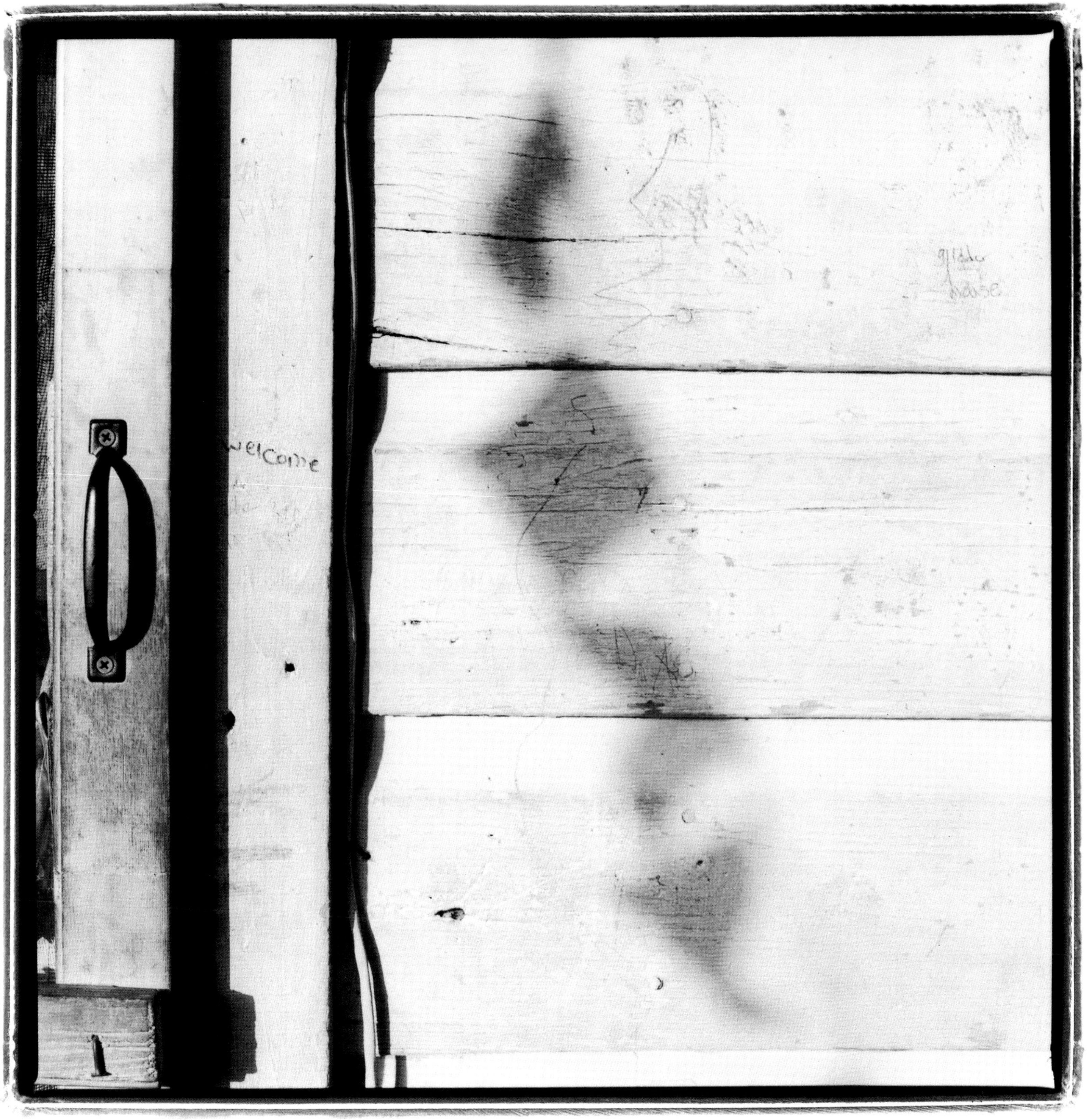
welcome

Weeping

UNIVERSITY OF TEXAS PRESS AUSTIN

Foreword by Anne Wilkes Tucker

Mary

Photographs by O. Rufus Lovett

Publication of this book was aided by the generous support of the University of Texas Press Advisory Council and Richard and Martha Rorschach.

Printed in China
First edition, 2006

Requests for permission to reproduce material from this work should be sent to:
Permissions
University of Texas Press
P.O. Box 7819
Austin, TX 78713-7819
www.utexas.edu/utpress/about/bpermission.html

♾ The paper used in this book meets the minimum requirements of ANSI/NISO Z39.48-1992 (R1997) (Permanence of Paper).

Library of Congress Cataloging-in-Publication Data

Lovett, O. Rufus, 1952–
Weeping Mary / O. Rufus Lovett ; foreword by Anne Wilkes Tucker.— 1st ed.
p. cm.
ISBN-13: 978-0-292-70932-4 (cloth : alk. paper)
ISBN-10: 0-292-70932-3 (alk. paper)
1. Weeping Mary (Tex.)—Pictorial works.
2. Weeping Mary (Tex.)—Social life and customs—Pictorial works. I. Title.

F394.W4L68 2006
976.4'141—dc22

2006006553

Book and jacket design by DJ Stout and Julie Savasky, Pentagram Design, Austin, Texas

Contents

Church Shadows

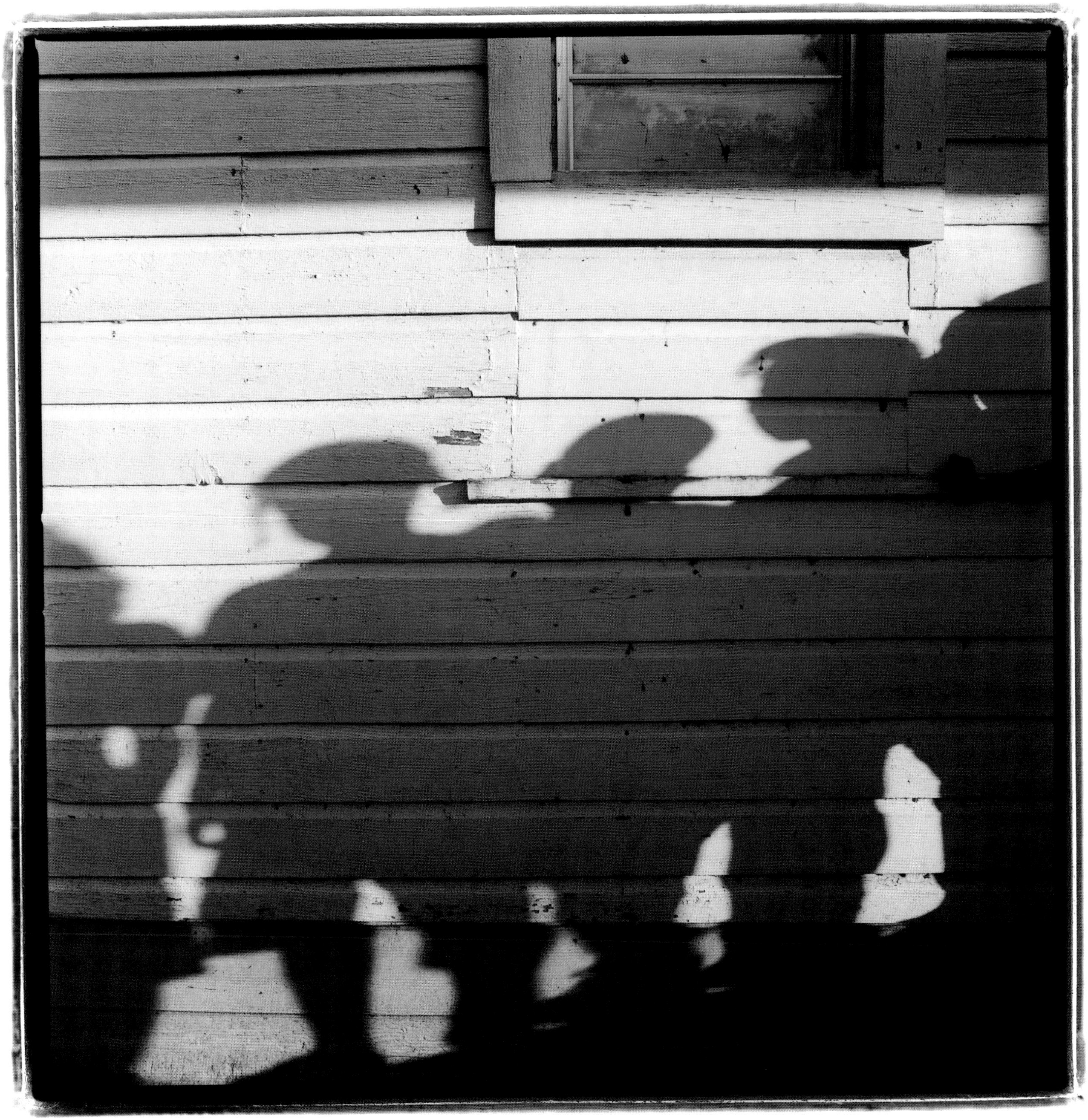

Weeping Mary It was spring in 1965 near the Pea River in Alabama. My father was driving along when he noticed a woman toting a fruit jar of well water to her husband who was plowing a mule in a nearby cornfield. As my dad pulled up to the corn rows, he began a smooth rap revealing his kind and honest persona that no doubt allowed him a brief but sincere entry into the lives of his newly found photographic subjects. The woman was at first hesitant about her husband and herself being portrayed in their work clothes in the field with the mule and plow. My father assured her that it would be a picture that would not be made fun of, and they agreed to be photographed. • Aside from his awareness of the beautiful light falling on their faces, and the translucency of the drinking water, and the gestures that reveal their strength, and his composition and careful cropping of the animals so they would remain a secondary notion within the frame, it is the unobtrusive, noninvasive presence of this white, blond, blue-eyed stranger that remains so remarkable. He had become a part of that picture: a self-portrait, so to speak, reflecting his own background. It revealed where he is from and what he is. He knew those people, and those animals, and the trees and the sky. A true kinship emerged. • My father's photographic experience on that one afternoon created a path that I have chosen to follow.

Twenty-nine Years Later It was spring in 1994 in East Texas and my writer friend Gary Borders said, "There's a place called Weeping Mary." What? "There's a place called Weeping Mary." Weeping Mary, where? "Down in Cherokee County, and you ought to check it out," he said. • That's how it all started: the photographs in this book, I mean. The name is so beautiful, and I've been thinking of that name since the day he first spoke it. • Weeping Mary is a small community that I have heard dates back to post–Civil War days, hidden in a river-bottom flat within the East Texas piney woods. Folklore has it that an African-American lady landowner named Mary was tricked out of selling her land to a wealthy white man. The white man had used a black man to purchase the land for him without Mary's knowing that the white man would become the property owner. This deceitful act upset Mary so much that she wept and wept and became known as Weeping Mary. Later the church and the community were named Weeping Mary. I've heard slightly different versions of the story, and I have read that perhaps the community was named for Mary Magdalene, who wept for Jesus, or that perhaps it was derived from a Catholic Church name, Our Lady of Sorrows. I am partial to the former legend about Mary who lost her land. • The children here grow up to graduate from schools, work for the highway department, the local forestry service, or sawmills, and stay in Weeping Mary raising children of their own. Their lives are intertwined with those of parents, grandparents, cousins, aunts, uncles, and neighbors, reflecting limited conditions enlightened by play and laughter and hope. At least for now the future is theirs to dream about and, perhaps, to fulfill. • It is through visualization of the community that I wish to recognize the importance of the lives of these children and their influences. By interpreting Weeping Mary, it is my goal to continue not only to comment on the people but also on their environment in terms of their relationship to it — how they are married to this place which is theirs and appears to stand still, but which subtly moves forward with the rest of the world in the twenty-first century. O. Rufus Lovett

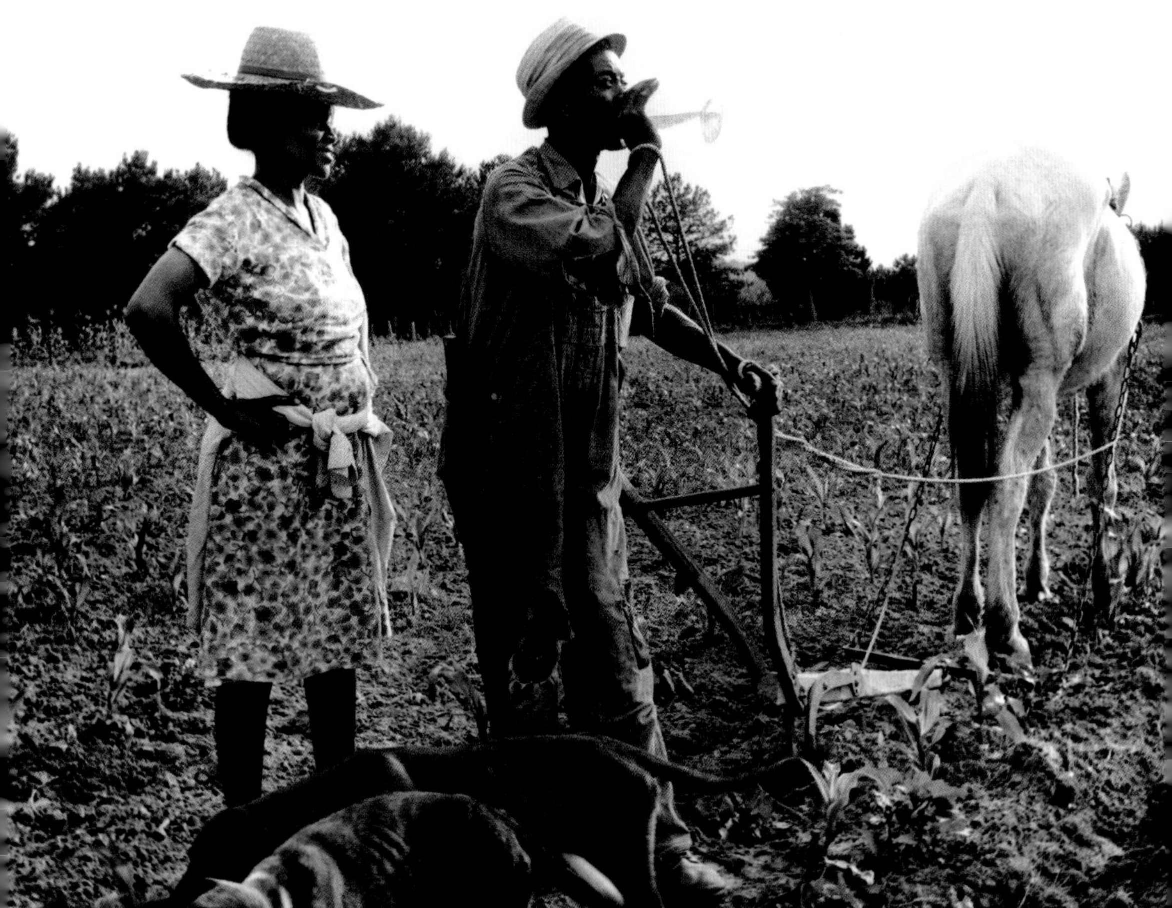

Photograph by Opal Rufus Lovett, Southeast Alabama, 1965

To my mother, Opal Dolores;

my father, Opal Rufus;

and my sister, Opal Dienitiza.

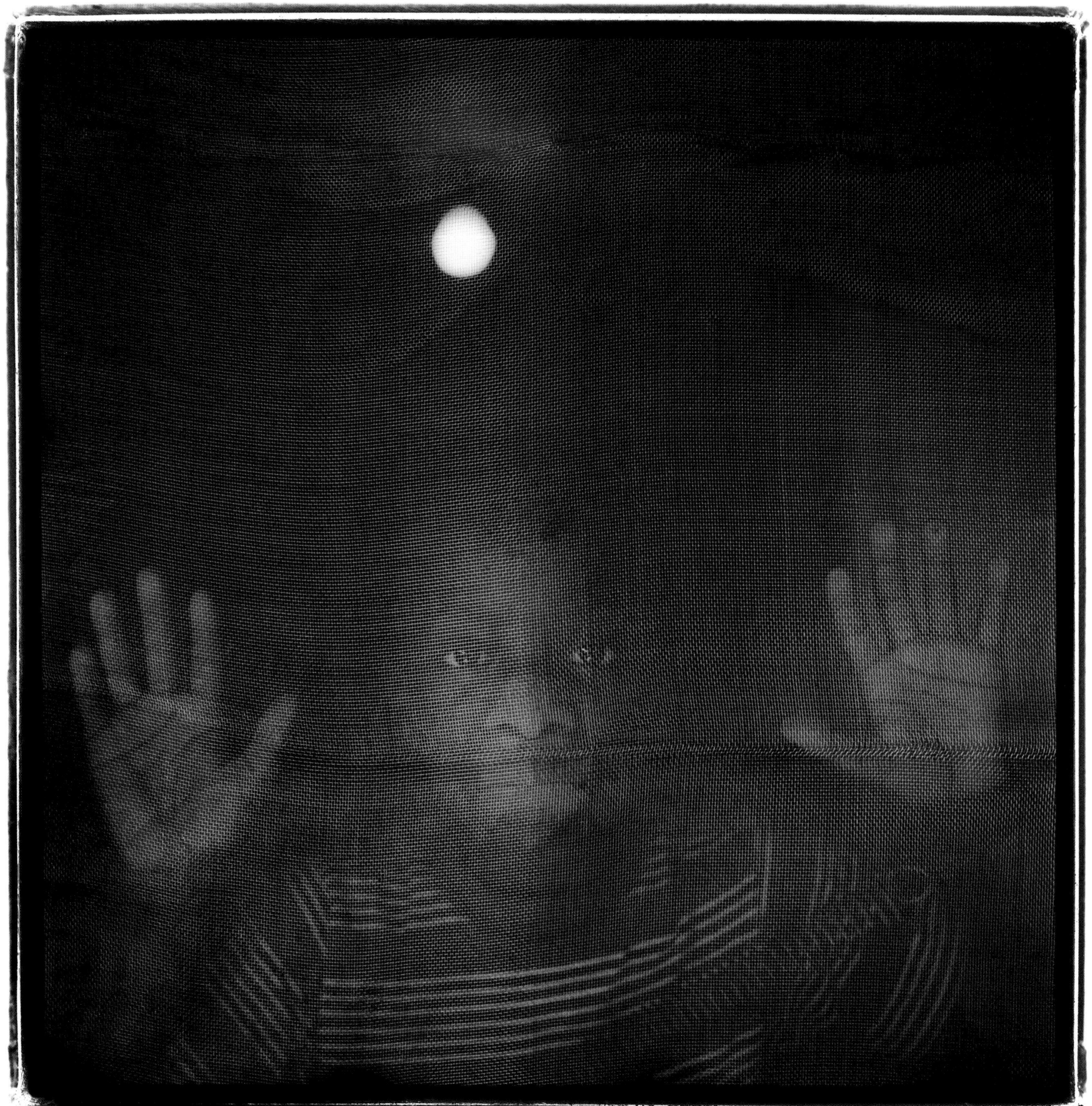

15

Screen Door

Pandora's Box

This is where we live. This is all we have.
Mrs. Parker

You've been coming here, but I don't know you.
John Parker, Mrs. Parker's grown son

I love to make pictures of people and I love this place.
O. Rufus Lovett

It was the name that first drew O. Rufus Lovett to Weeping Mary, Texas. At the time, he had been teaching photography at Kilgore College, a two-year school in East Texas, for seventeen years (as of this writing, he has been there nearly twenty-eight years) and simultaneously working for various magazines, most frequently *Texas Monthly*. Previously, his most widely known picture story had been an evolving one on the Kilgore Rangerettes, the legendary Kilgore College dance drill team that has performed throughout Texas and in many U.S. and foreign venues. His photographs of the Rangerettes were first published in *Texas Monthly* in 1990, and most recently republished in September 2004 in an article that included twenty-six photographs spread over eight pages, plus the magazine cover.[1] In today's magazine world, few photo essays receive that many pages, but *Texas Monthly* rightly understood that the Rangerettes are a beloved Texas tradition and that Lovett's pictures vividly capture the girls' distinctive high kicks, long lines of precision dancing, relentlessly cheerful smiles, and status as unofficial Texas ambassadors.

Like the Rangerettes, Weeping Mary has a long history in East Texas. There are many stories about its origins, but most agree that freed slaves founded the community just after the Civil War. The black population of Texas was freed by the declaration of Yankee Major General Gordon Granger on June 19, 1865, and this date, which has become known as Juneteenth, is an official Texas holiday, celebrated by parades, speeches, and concerts, as well as by—in Weeping Mary and throughout the state—barbecues and picnics. In 1865, there were about a quarter of a million slaves in Texas, who, when freed, had nothing of their own and few opportunities to make a living. Many turned to agriculture as a way to scrape out a living and remain independent. This led to settlements like Weeping Mary, which never was, an is not now, a prosperous community. There are almost no job there, so people commute to nearby towns to work in nursin homes or sawmills, or for government departments. But th neighbors are tight-knit, many are related, and the citizens ar proud of their 140-year legacy.

Modern-day Weeping Mary is a small and unincorporate neighborhood of approximately 250 people living in maybe fort houses; the population varies from weekday to weekend as siblings and children return home from jobs in other communities The community is situated west of the intersection of east-wes Texas Highway 21 and north-south Texas Highway 69 and down two-lane road, and the Weeping Mary Baptist Church is the firs building visible on approach. The church is relatively new, well kept and prominently located. From the 1890s until World War II there was a school in the community, but children are now buse to schools in Alto, down Route 21. On the other side of the bridge just past the church, tight clusters of houses make up the rest o the community's buildings. The layout is not a traditional suburba plan, with each house on a distinct and well-defined lot. Clearly over the years, new houses have been built and some trailers hav been moved in between existing houses. Front and backyards ar communal, as is the land around barbecue pits and what suffice as playgrounds. Some residences have well-established flowerbed or vegetable gardens. Hanging baskets decorate many porches and the front of Mrs. Martin's house is almost hidden behind he trellised roses.

On the day I visited Weeping Mary, a Saturday in late April 2005 residents were gathered in small groups: a mother and son talkin behind her house, men drinking beers around a smoking barbecue children playing on a front porch, and women in their living room cooling themselves in front of electric window fans. A young woma wove cornrows into a friend's hair in her open-air, impromptu beauty parlor, exactly as she wove hair extensions on another da in Lovett's photograph "Extensions."

Gary Borders, publisher of the Lufkin, Texas, newspaper, th *Lufkin Daily News*, and the person who first introduced Lovett t Weeping Mary, refers to the community as being "Behind Th Pine Curtain."[2] It's both an actual description, because a grea many of the trees in East Texas are some variety of pine, and reference to the north-south, botanical divide that separates Eas Texas from the rest of the state in vegetation as well as in cultur nd economy. East Texas is the dampest region of Texas, with ayous crisscrossing dense forests. It hosts the Big Thicket National Preserve and four national forests (Sam Houston, Davy Crockett, Angelina, and Sabine), as well as the Alabama and Coushatta Indian reservations and the internationally recognized Tyler Rose Garden. Tyler supplies one-third of the rose bushes grown in the United States, a fact which is not compatible with he image of Texas that immediately comes to mind for most people inside and outside the state.

Beaumont is the largest city between Houston and the Louisiana border, and towns north of Beaumont range from hose with populations of a few hundred, such as Weeping Mary, o the city of Tyler with 100,000 residents. Like the rest of Texas, East Texas has its share of oil wells. In fact, the first Texas oil well was drilled near Nacogdoches in 1865. However, there was no ollow-through after this discovery. The true oil boom began in October 1930 when oil was discovered in Spindletop, Texas, eading to the development of the vast East Texas oil field. Dairy cattle are another important source of income in East Texas, rather than the beef cattle that sustain West Texas. But logging s the most important local industry. Cherokee County, which ncludes Weeping Mary, is forested on over 50 percent of its land. Such lushness also provides ample wildlife to fish and hunt, as one can see in Lovett's photographs.

First attracted by its name, Lovett began to photograph the close-knit rural community of Weeping Mary, about 100 miles from his home in Longview, in 1994. The strength of the community mpressed him, and he felt a kinship with it; it reminded him of places and people he knew as a boy in Alabama. He approached he townspeople slowly, not even bringing out his camera on the irst few visits. Since then he has returned repeatedly to talk to he residents, particularly some of the older women, and to continue to photograph them—especially the children, many of whom have grown into young adulthood in front of his lens. The children were the first to accept Lovett and his camera without suspicion, and they soon became his most common subject. He relishes their moods, ranging from joy to vulnerability to sweetness o curiosity. Their innocence comes through, and the openness of their emotions, such as those of the boy Kentavious, seen with broad tear-tracks down his cheeks. However, the presence of a protective arm around the child's shoulder checks whatever concerns may arise in the viewer. In fact, it's clear from Lovett's pictures that children are never far from the watchful eyes of adults—sitting on porches, on parked cars, or in old metal chairs in the yard, or looking through screened windows and doors. Unlike in houses now sealed by air conditioning throughout the South, air and sounds flow easily through these interiors.

When the children are in Weeping Mary, they are far from the organized playgrounds of schools. There are no nearby malls in which to wander, and no drugstore or movie theater in which to congregate. They race their bicycles on dirt roads or in communal yards, play hide-and-seek at the church door, or imagine a porch rail to be a wild pony, with a pillow wired to the rail as a substitute saddle. Occasionally, a trampoline will go up, a plastic pool will appear, or a makeshift softball field will be carved temporarily out of a pasture. The town is not without modern technologies: Computers and televisions sit in living rooms. Cell phones are attached to belts. Blaring radios initiate dancing. Other signs of the world outside include school trophies on a window ledge and Superman on a T-shirt. But one cannot help sensing a simplicity reminiscent of a bygone era.

Another extended series within Lovett's Weeping Mary project is the yard art that appears at Christmas, although only a couple of the pictures are reproduced here.[3] Like any folk artists, these residents start with the materials at hand, such as a bicycle mounted on two posts and decorated with ropes of small lights. If one lighted Santa Claus figure is festive, several versions of Santa grouped together seems to be preferable. On some houses, patterns created by strings of Christmas lights extend past the lines formed by roofs and doors. In Weeping Mary, Lovett records star patterns and abstract rhythms of light on exterior walls. The friendly competition from house to nearby house is another sign of the strength of the community and the active imaginations of the residents. Some of these photographs also fit into another ongoing series that Lovett calls "Southern Claus," in which he records an odd and uniquely Southern blend of lighted Santa Claus figures and masks that functions as both "a spiritual shrine and good ol' Southern commercial kitsch."[4] Each year Lovett selects a picture from this series as his Christmas card.

Lovett is well schooled in the history of photography. His teachers—John Beck at Sam Houston State University and Nolan Bailey at East Texas State University—exposed him to a wide range of the styles and genres that have been explored by other photographers. Plus, Lovett worked two summers with the master landscape photographer Ansel Adams, himself a great source of information and opinion about his predecessors and contemporaries in photography's brief 160-year history.[5] Lovett's resume reveals that he frequently seeks out other photographers—both commercial and fine art—to attend their lectures and workshops and continue the learning process. Like every good teacher, Lovett also learns from the process of selecting historical images to show his students.

The list of photographers who most influenced his work is eclectic. Besides the Farm Security Administration photographers from the 1930s and 1940s (particularly Dorothea Lange and Russell Lee), other photographers that he lists as important include Henri Cartier-Bresson, Helen Levitt, Robert Frank, Gordon Parks, and Elliot Erwitt. None of these choices is surprising, given his love of documentary photography. But then he adds landscape photographers Adams and Edward Weston, portrait photographer Arnold Newman, and abstractionist Aaron Siskind. Lovett explains that all of them reflect on the human condition in the best of their work. He continued, "It's a theme that allows the photographer to cross many boundaries regarding documentary, interpretive portraiture, still life, and art. The variety of possibilities attracts me and drives me to work in this genre."[6] The influence of Adams and Weston is most evident in the beauty of his prints with their rich tonal range. Because Weeping Mary is situated in a low area and is well shaded with trees, and because many of the house interiors are dark, getting sufficient light to properly expose his negatives is difficult. This difficulty makes the richness of his prints all the more admirable.

Lovett's approach to Weeping Mary is not that of a historian or a sociologist. His titles are brief; subjects are not identified by name. We can't easily connect the boy in "Wild Hog Diptych" with the same boy seen four years later in "Cousins." Lovett favors close-ups and details, not wide-angle views that would put activities in a greater context. He loves the play of light on skin and fabrics with lush floral patterns, and he uses flash to heighten the contrasting values. His pictures are more poetic than narrative and tend to evoke a viewer's imagination or, perhaps, a sympathetic recollection of the viewer's own childhood. The images are not site-specific enough to allow another photographer to locate where Lovett stood when he made certain pictures, or to allow a historian to create a model of the neighborhood just by using these images. We can't perceive on our own—and he doesn't instruct us in the titles or texts—that what appear to be three different screen doors on three different houses are different doors on the same house over time. Trees have been cut down; one house burned. Some o the people in the pictures have moved away and a few have died Lovett doesn't trace the complex lines of family relationships nor has he tried to photograph every resident systematically Thus, while he has visited frequently with Mr. and Mrs. Parker he rarely sees their son John Parker (hence, Parker's quote at the beginning of this essay). No documentary photographer can cove every detail of a complex project, and the best ones don't try Rather, they trust their vision and instincts. It is the spirit o the community that interests Lovett, rather than the litera appearance or chronology of events.

Lovett's pictures are richly interpretive. To fully understan the degree of his intervention in what we see, it is important to think about what he excludes as well as about what catches his eye One can see that people, more than places or objects, sustain his interest, although neither of the latter is neglected. He also prefers close-ups to vistas, and relishes the great wealth of human gestures with which we express ourselves. Repeatedly—in his pictures made in China, on the streets of Houston, in Kilgore, and in Weeping Mary—Lovett concentrates on postures and body-part details. In the Weeping Mary series, look at how lovingly Cherry holds his wallet open to the photographs of his now-grown children, and how dressing up for Sunday services seems to quiet the usually exuberant girls. In "Porch Shoes," a woman sits relaxing in an old chair with her beer, palmetto leaf fan, and cigarettes tucked within easy reach around her body and her bare feet dangling ove the floor. In other pictures, Lovett focuses on a bejeweled hand elaborate hairdos, a narrow dress strap stretched across a woman's smooth, round shoulder, and the utter peace of a sleeping child He shoots and prints without much manipulation of the photographic materials, but he is highly selective in what he does and does not choose to photograph.

Until recently, there wasn't a sign marking the exit to Weeping Mary off Highway 21. Since this project began, Lovett has published two articles on Weeping Mary in the *Daily Sentinel*, one in *Texas* magazine in the Sunday edition of the *Houston Chronicle* one in the Blue Sky Gallery magazine, and one in *Texas Monthly* He has also exhibited the photographs in various venues in Texas and Alabama. These shows and articles have led others to the once happily neglected community. While the residents have rown to trust Lovett, they have been angered by the insensitivity f some who have been attracted to Weeping Mary by his photo-raphs. Someone wrote a play that was performed in New York, nd another person wrote a children's mystery book titled *immering Secrets in Weeping Mary.* One woman who writes for the *'herokeean Herald* in Rusk, Texas, drove around photographing ·ithout asking permission, and in the process captured a few esidents who had specifically asked not to have their pictures aken. Then she published those pictures with an article that ontained inaccuracies that angered the residents. Lovett has espected all requests that he not take a picture, but as John 'arker commented about the intruding strangers, "You have tarted something that can't be stopped."[7]

A photographer's curiosity about the world and desire to see nd to record could be likened to that of Pandora, who was created y the Greek God Zeus and sent to earth. She was then tempted to pen a box, which, unbeknownst to her, contained misfortunes uch as diseases, sorrows, vices, and crimes that had not previously fflicted man. Once released from the box by Pandora, whose uriosity overwhelmed her judgment, the winged evil spirits lagued her and her husband and the rest of the world henceforth. y the same token, the dilemma of every responsible photojour-alist and documentary photographer is to weigh his or her uriosity and desire to photograph a situation against the rights f the subjects. It's hard, in the Internet age, to find a new subject, ne that has not been covered by other photographers or writers. Vhen a fresh subject, such as Weeping Mary, is discovered, and hen, as with Lovett, the photographer feels a strong personal esonance with the subject, it is hard to walk away. How does ne balance whatever harm the invasion of privacy might ause against the value of preserving something of beauty and uman relevance?

In one recent instance, the photographer Dave Anderson, ho was photographing in the devastated Ninth Ward of New)rleans after Hurricane Katrina, wrote, "I would have liked to ave taken portraits of folks, but could not bring myself to ask nore than a couple of people. I just didn't feel right. . . . People ere too traumatized. So my pics are almost exclusively of the estruction."[8] In Weeping Mary, Lovett's intentions are not to how deprivation or trauma or tragedy. He is an outsider, but he dmires this community. Given how much he respects the work f the photographers in the Farm Security Administration, Lovett's essay on Weeping Mary could have been more like their pictures. The FSA photographers sought to engage their audiences by revealing the social and economic plights of their subjects, in hopes of instigating social change that would improve the lives that they photographed. But the economic situation of most of Weeping Mary's residents isn't of interest to Lovett—and, had he focused on that aspect of their lives, he probably would not have been welcomed back repeatedly.

Lovett often quotes the English painter Francis Bacon, who wrote, "The contemplation of things as they are . . . is in itself a nobler thing than a whole harvest of invention." Lovett then goes on to say, "This statement is a justification of all the circum-stances that have been observed and then interpreted by the photographer in love with the nature of documentary photo-graphs."[9] The clarity of Lovett's pictures allows viewers to feel the same fascination with this community that drew him in. "O. Rufus Lovett," wrote John Hockenberry in *Life* magazine, "finds for us a world far from any center, and we feel relieved, swept away to a refuge. His images don't readily explain themselves, but they do implore us to sit awhile and stay, something of a miracle in itself."[10]

ANNE WILKES TUCKER
Gus and Lyndall Wortham Curator
The Museum of Fine Arts, Houston

NOTES

1. Katy Vine, text, and O. Rufus Lovett, photographs, "Alive and Kicking," *Texas Monthly*, September 2004, 114–121, 220–221.
2. Gary B. Borders, "Catching Up with My Old Friend Rufus," *Daily Sentinel*, March 7, 1999, 3C.
3. See Gary B. Borders, "Christmas in Weeping Mary," *Daily Sentinel*, December 25, 1994, 6A.
4. O. Rufus Lovett, "Off the Road a Little," an unpublished paper delivered at the Festival of Southern Autobiography at the University of Central Arkansas, 1998.
5. Ansel Adams Workshop, Yosemite, California, 1980 and 1981.
6. O. Rufus Lovett, "Off the Road a Little."
7. Unidentified man to O. Rufus Lovett and Anne Tucker, April 23, 2005.
8. Dave Anderson, e-mail to Anne Tucker, September 18, 2005.
9. O. Rufus Lovett, "Off the Road a Little."
10. "The 2000 Alfred Eisenstaedt Awards: The Best Magazine Photos of the Year," *Life*, Spring 2000, 10 and 42.

20

Chi Chi's Cousin

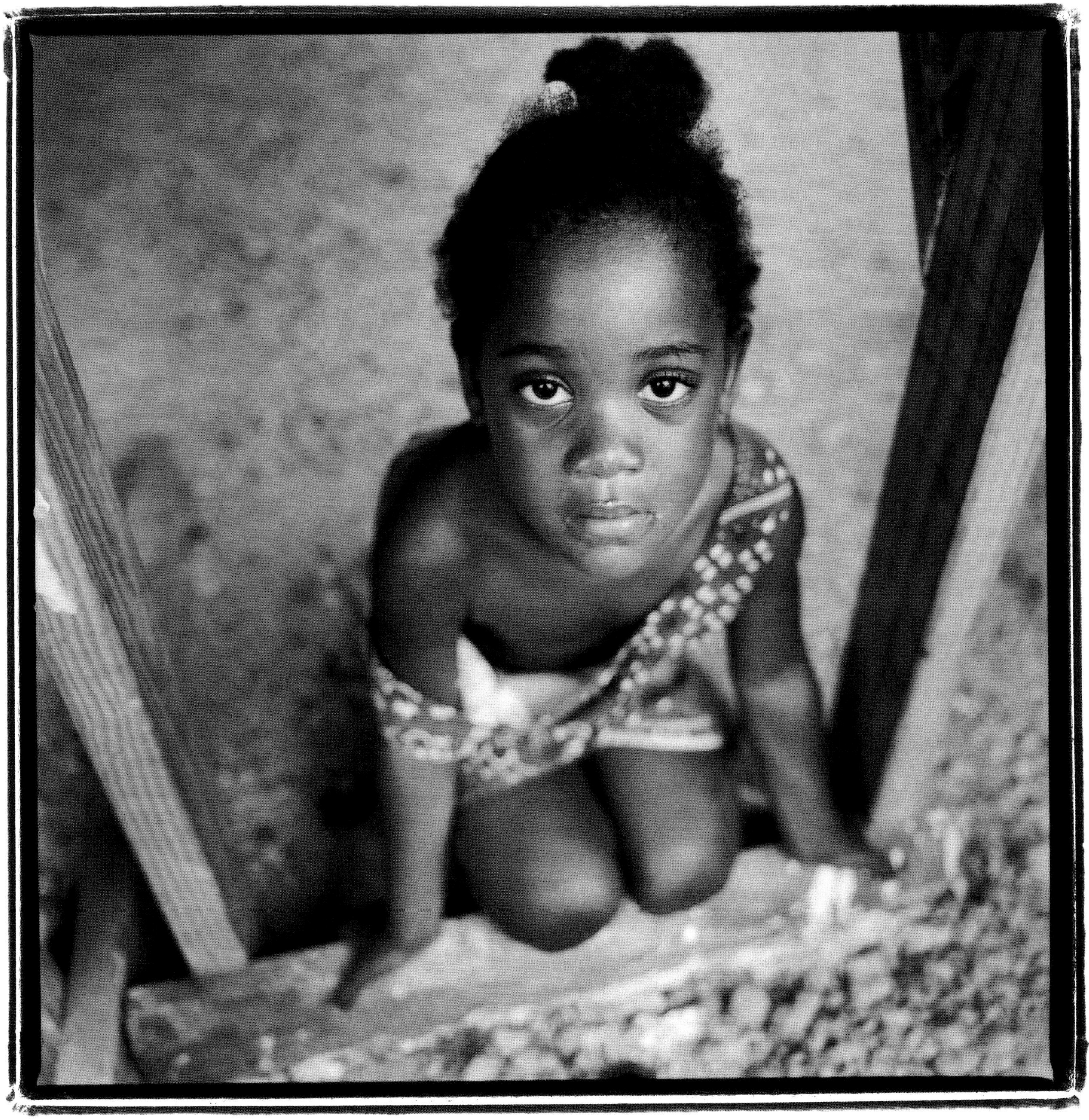

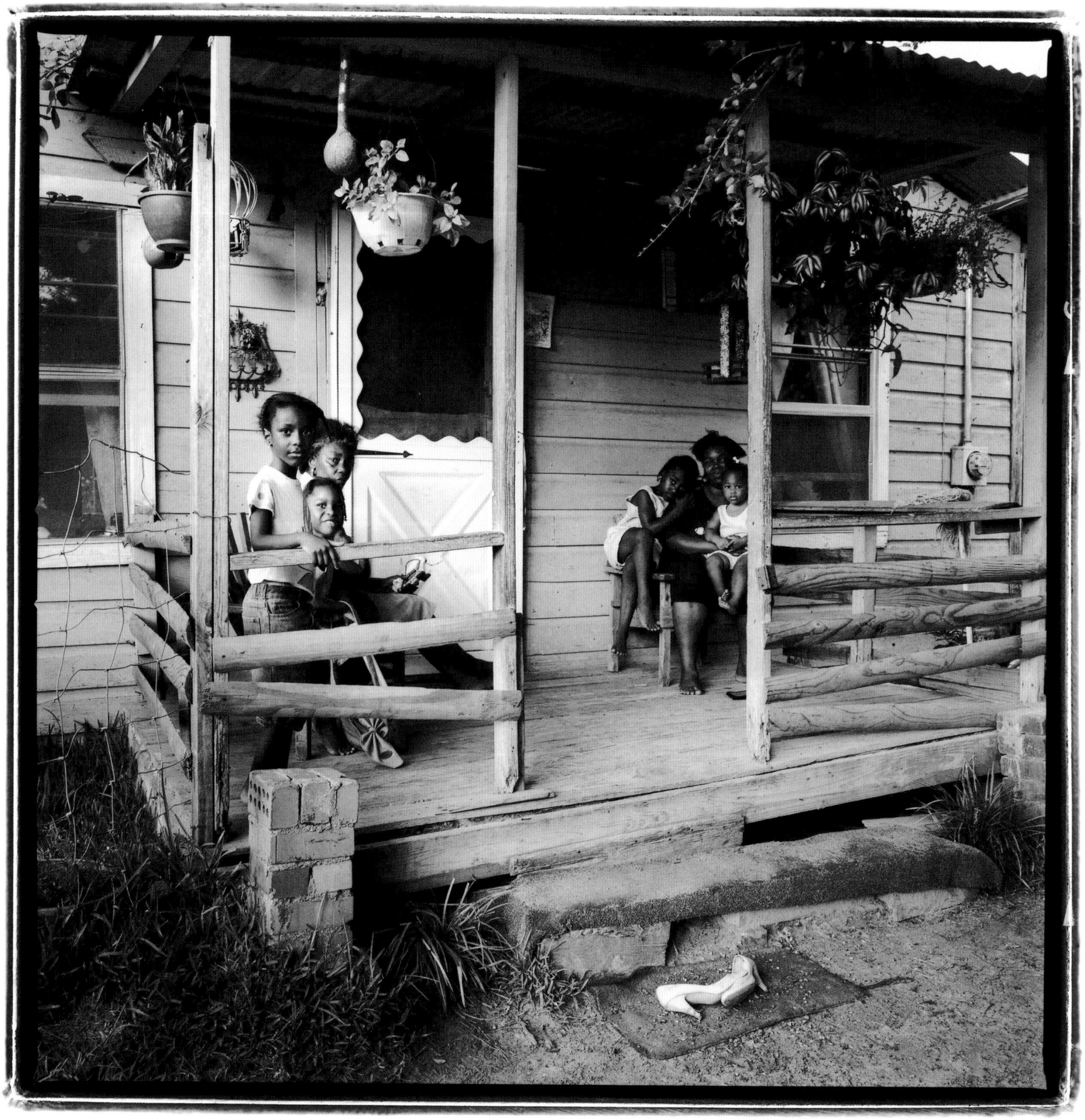

Mrs. Martin's Porch

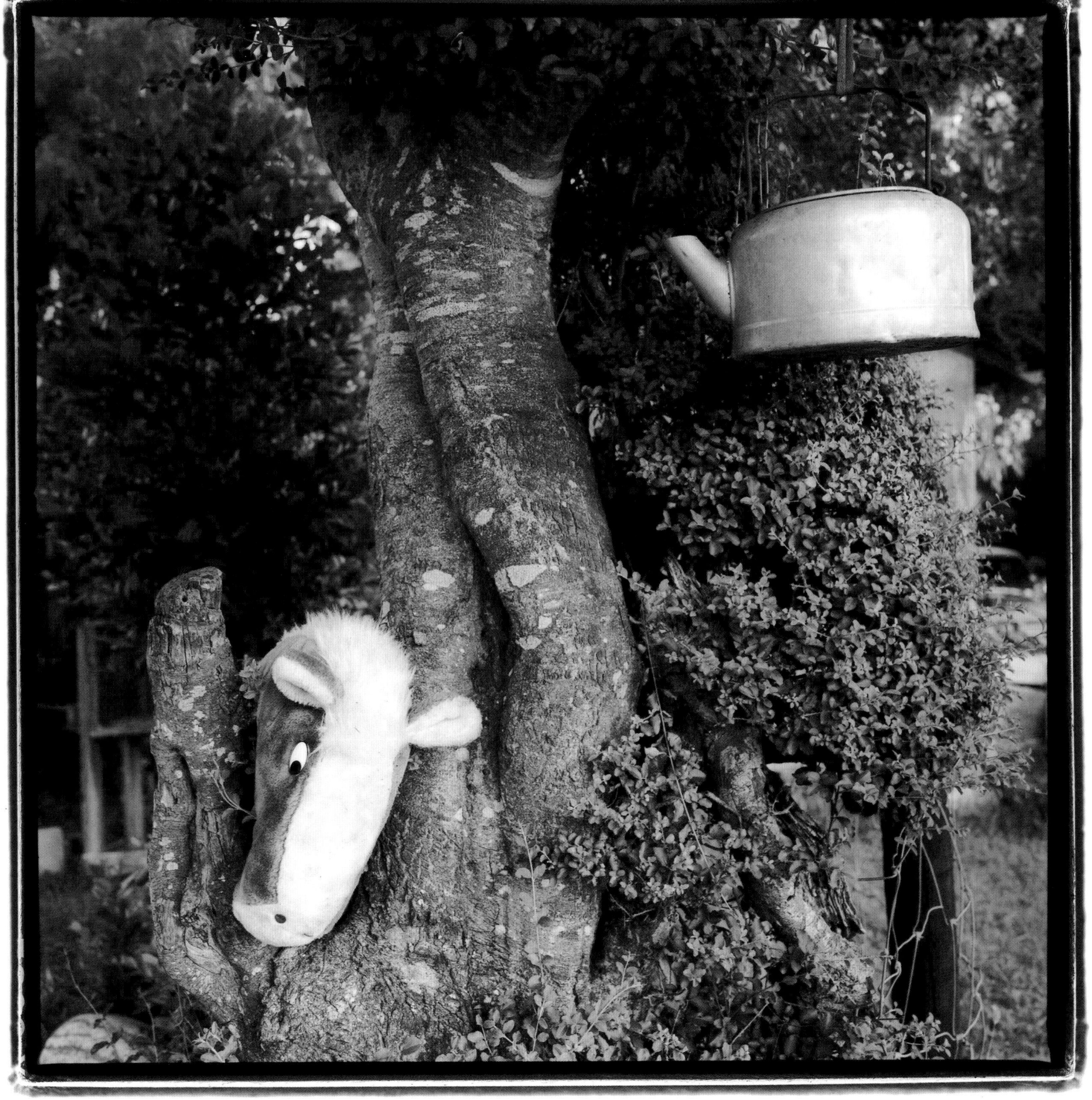

25

Mrs. Martin's Still Life

Porch Shoes

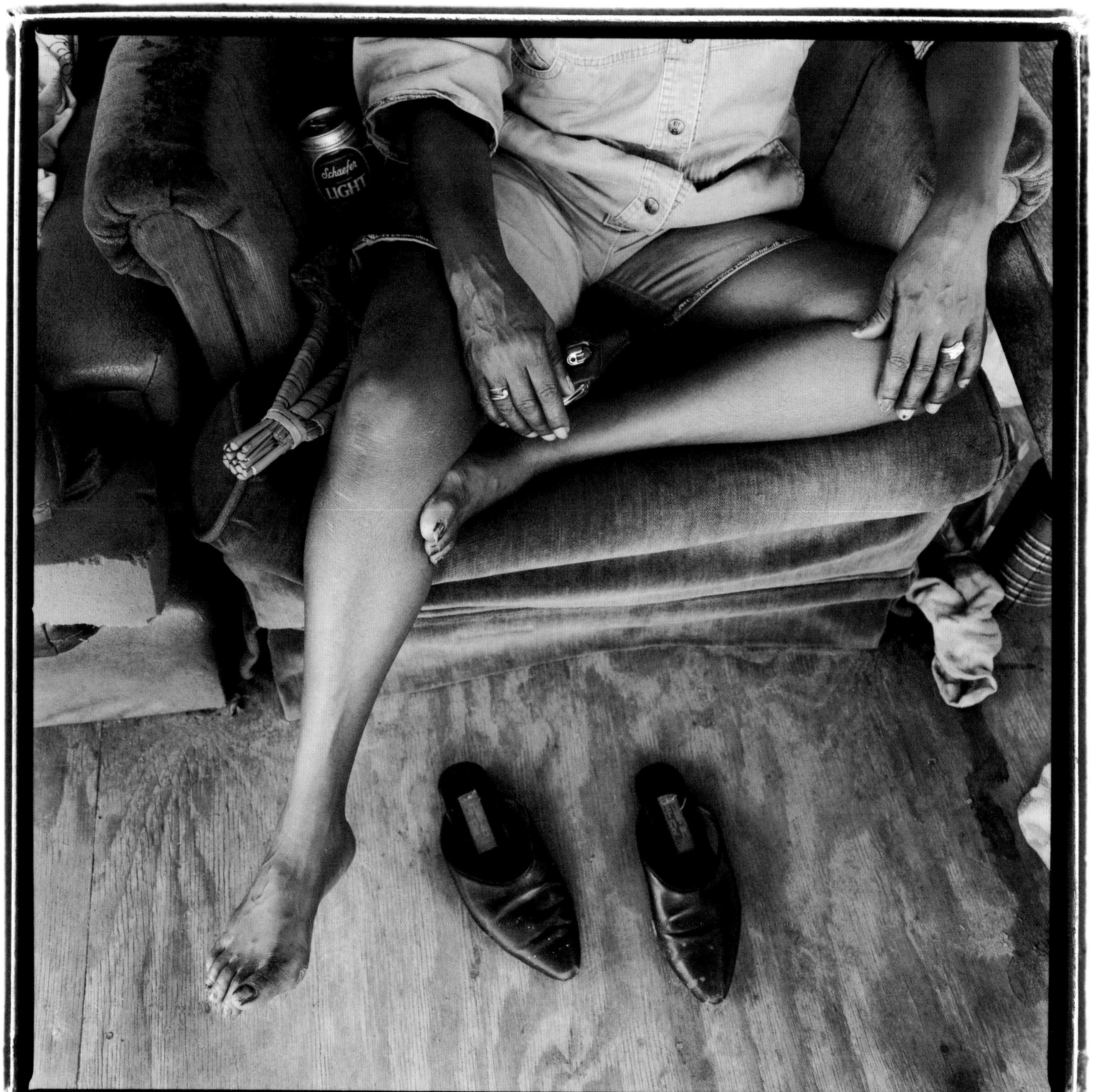
Schaefer
LIGHT

Eyes

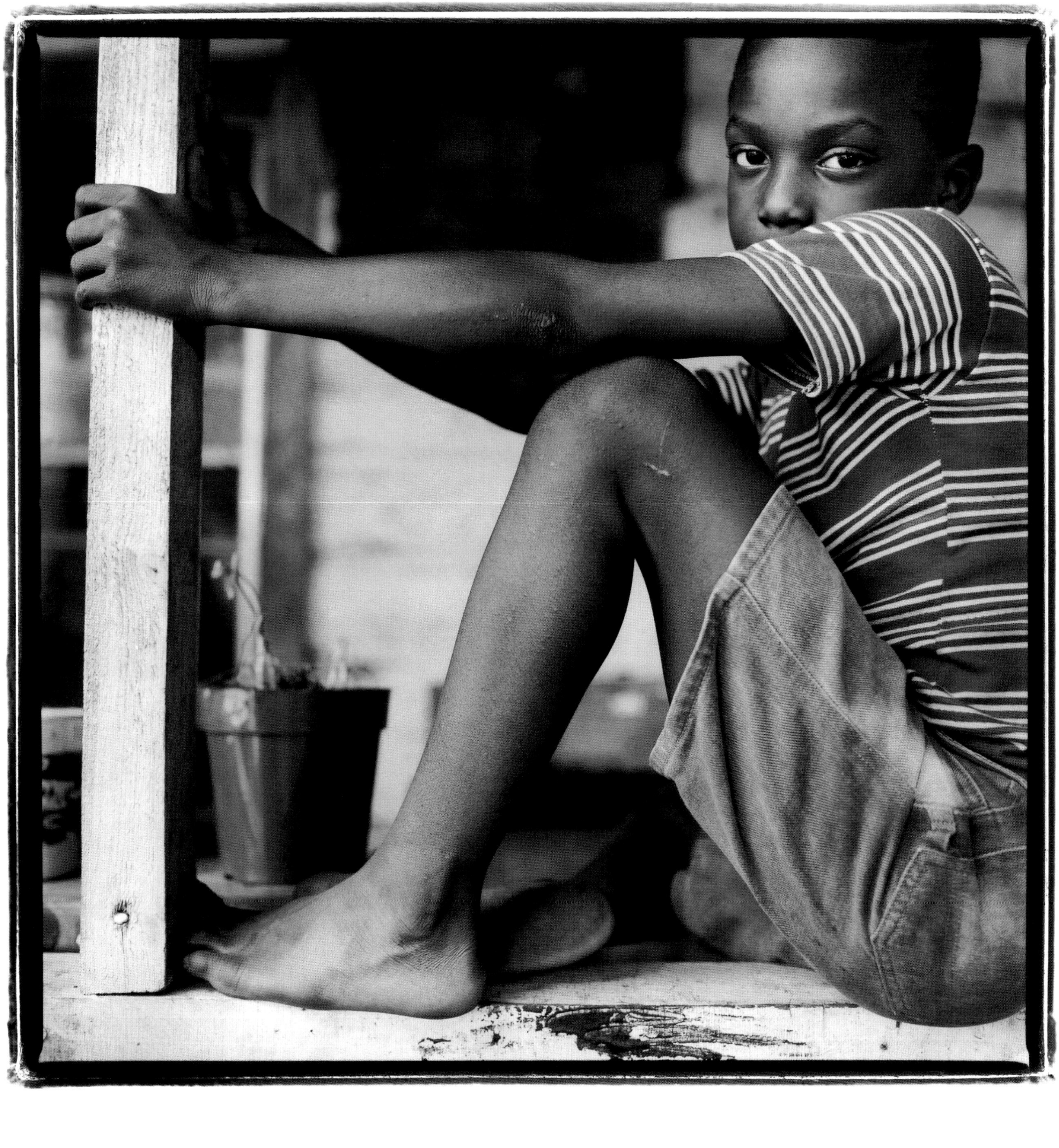

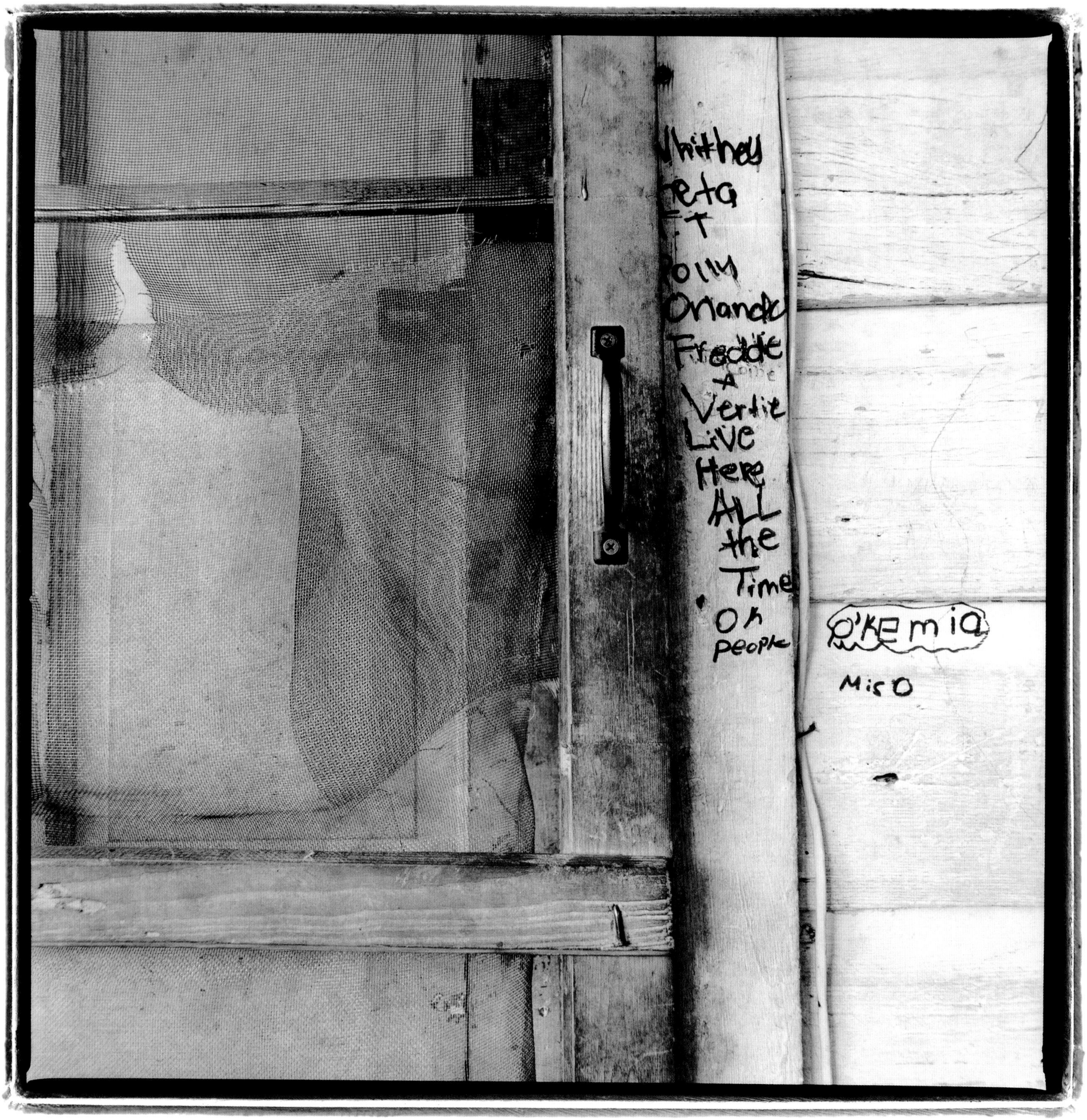
Vertie
Live
Here
ALL
the
Time
Oh
people

OK People

Spelling

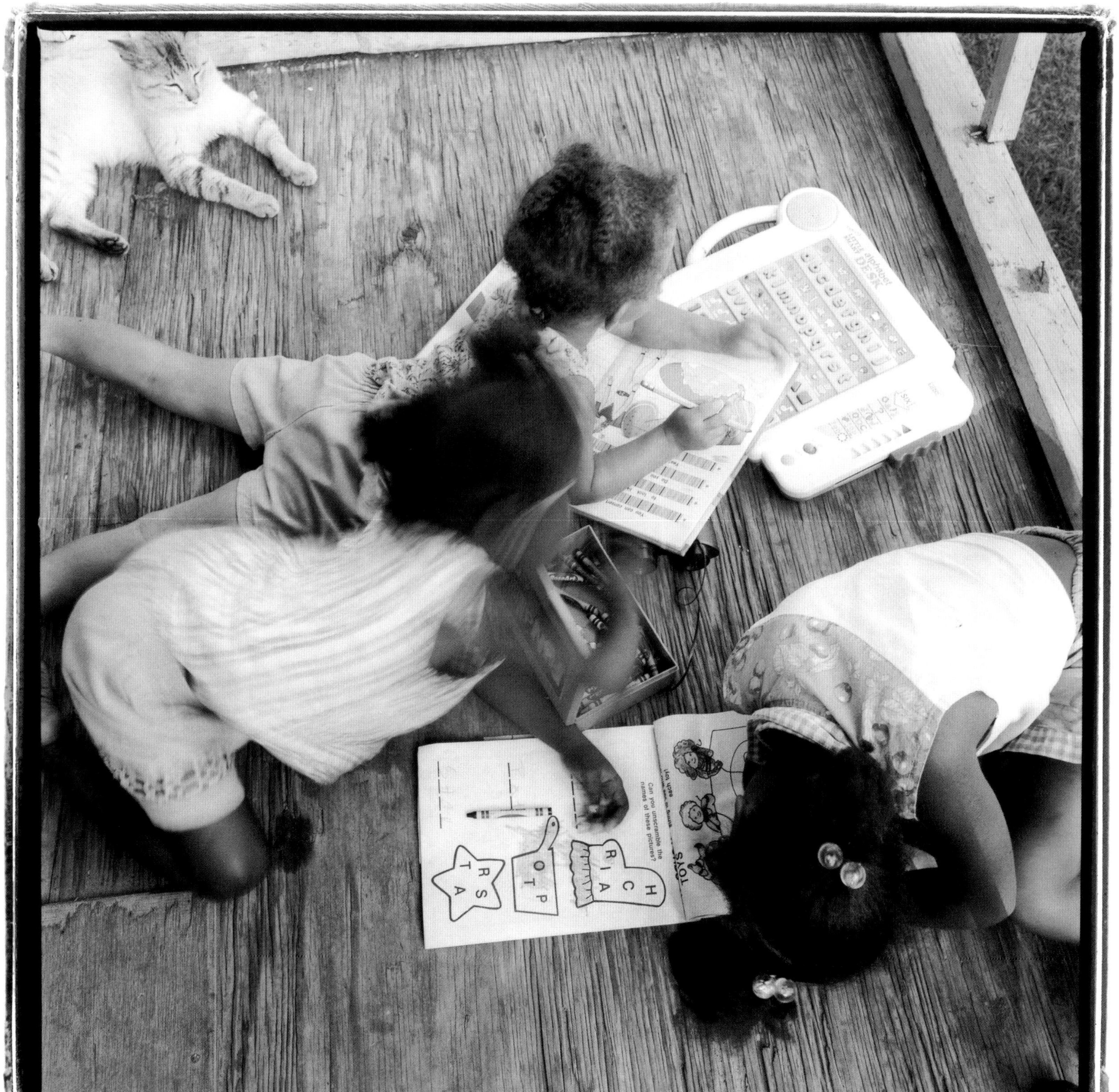

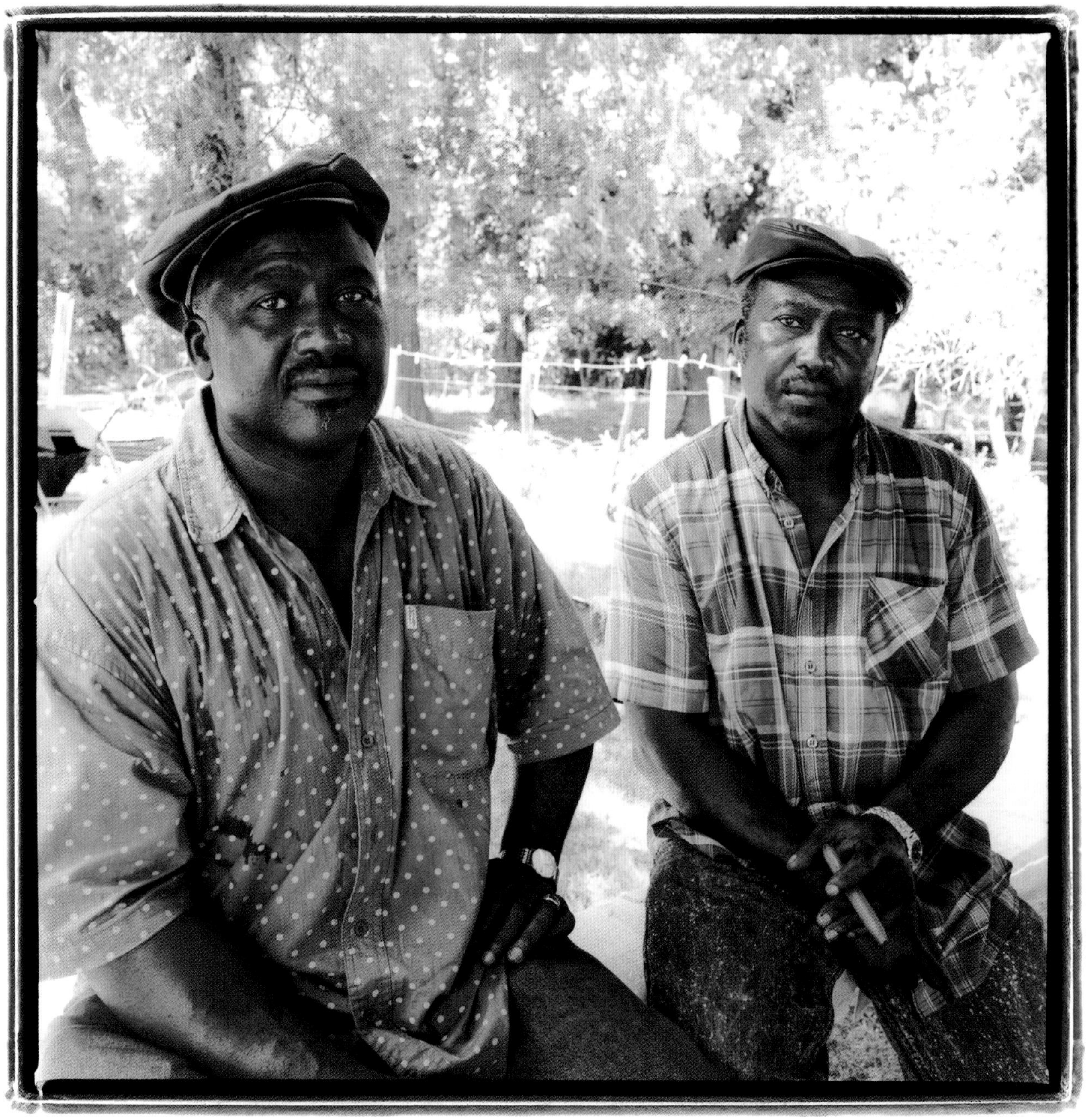

Twins

Twins

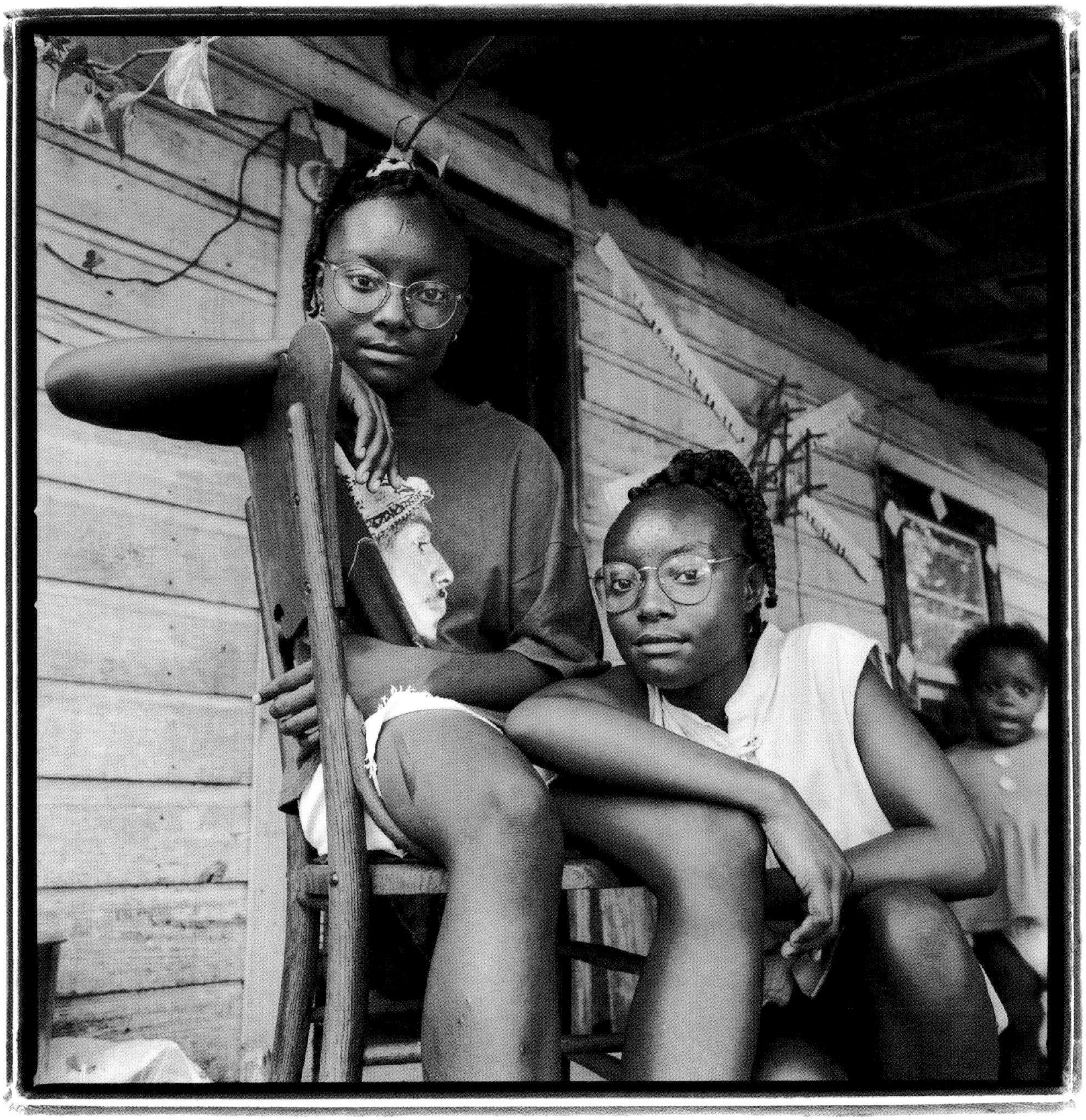

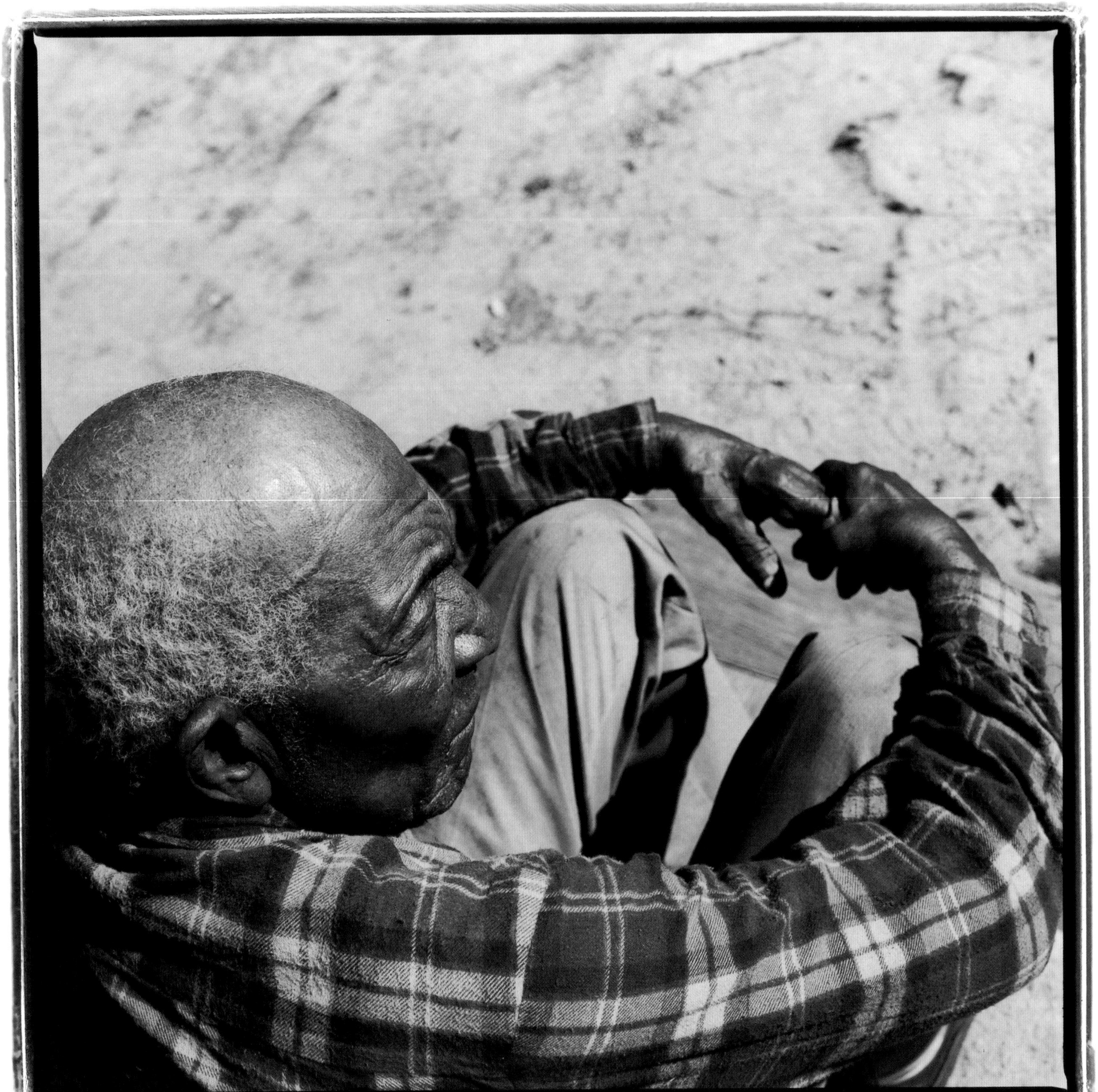

Uncle Bill

Cousins

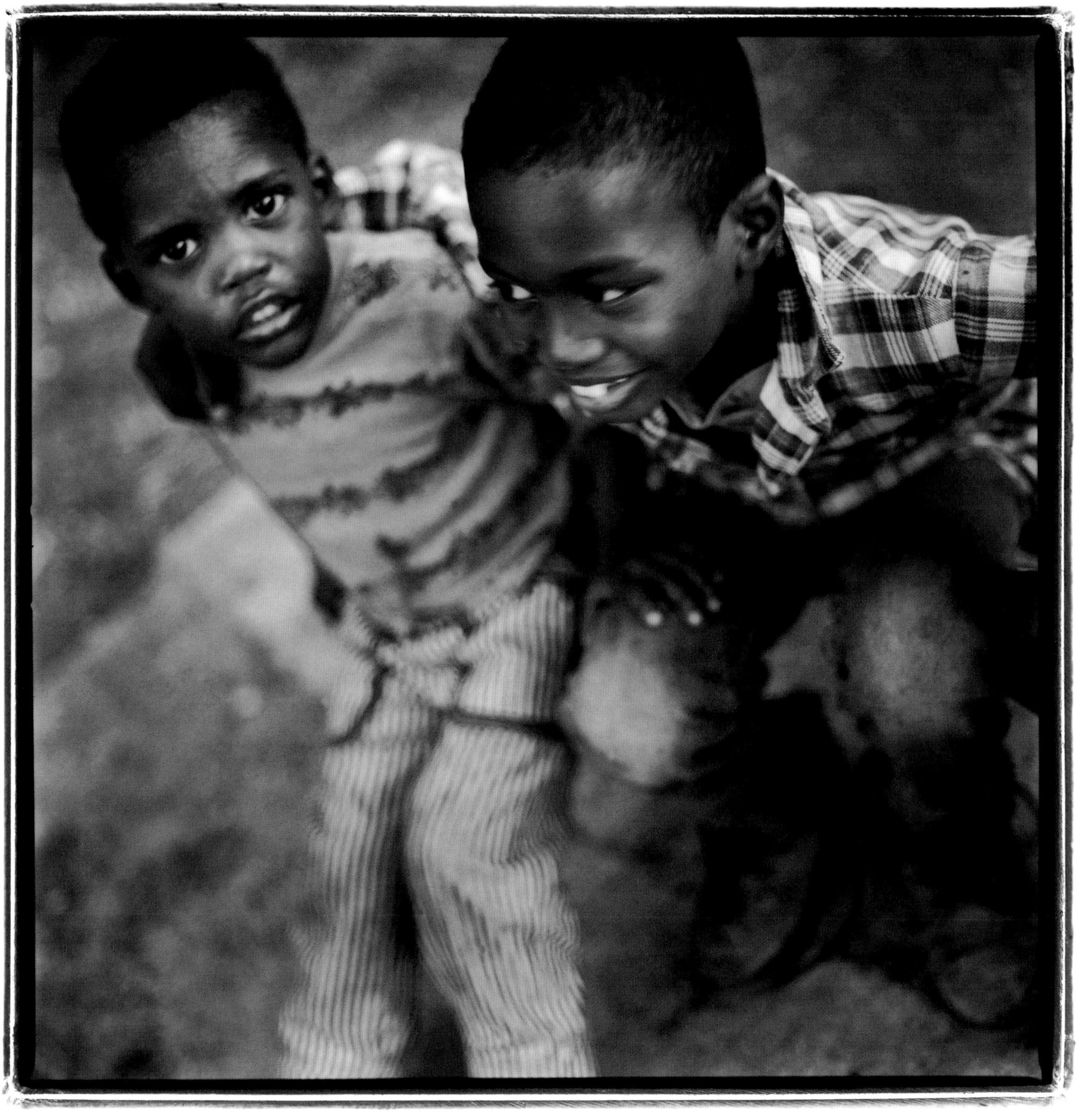

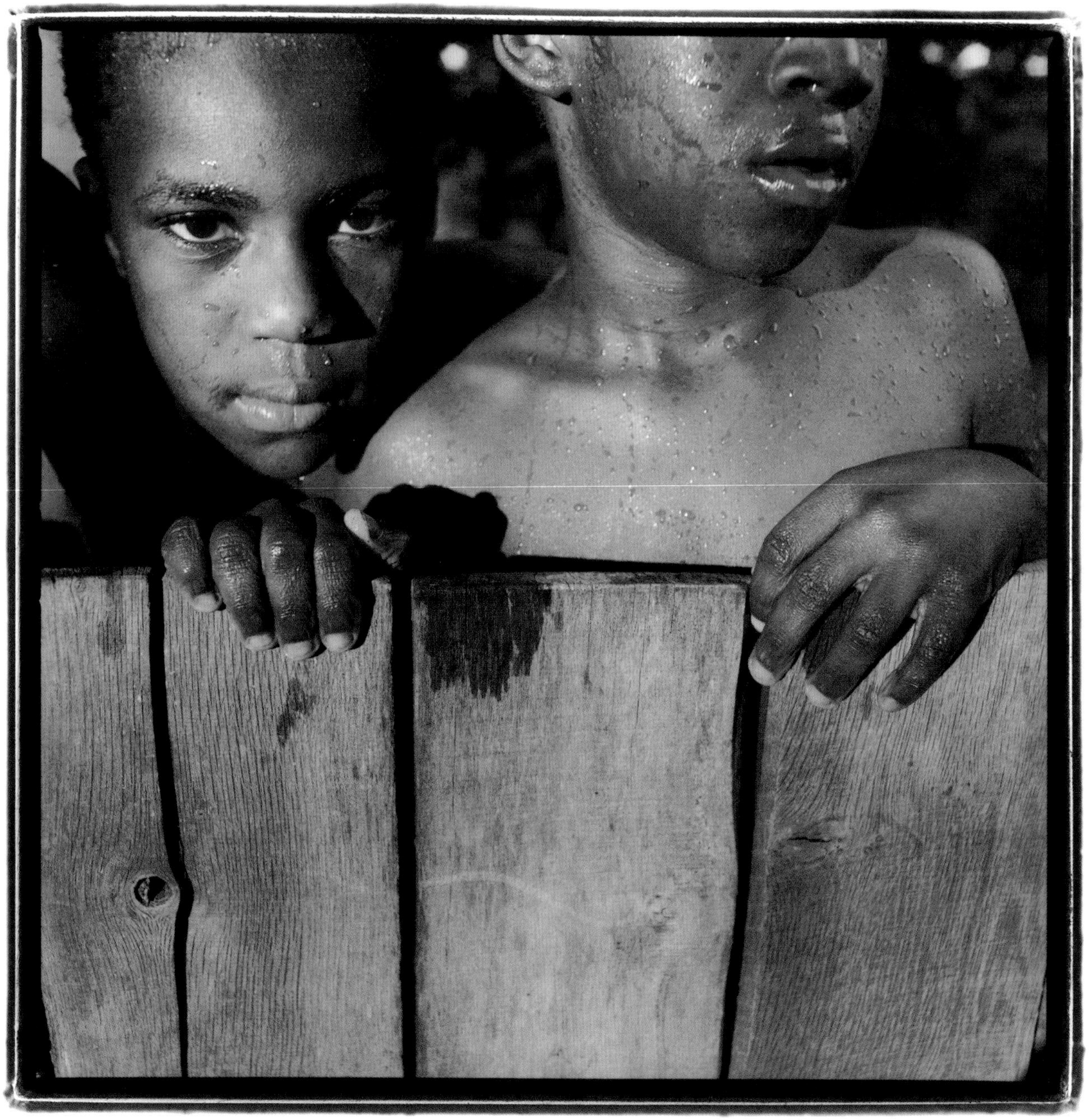

Swimmer's Fence

Swimmer's Fence

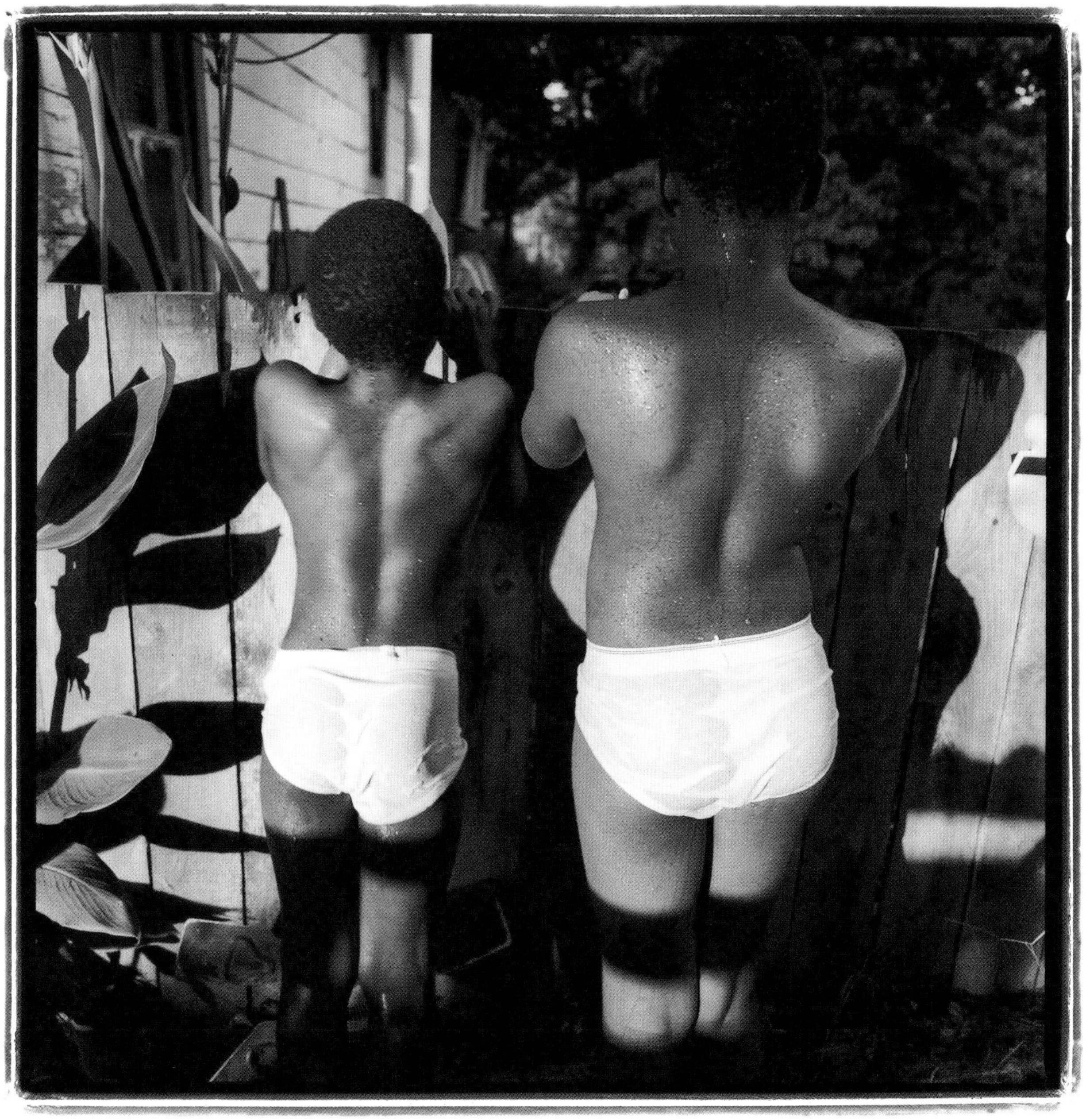

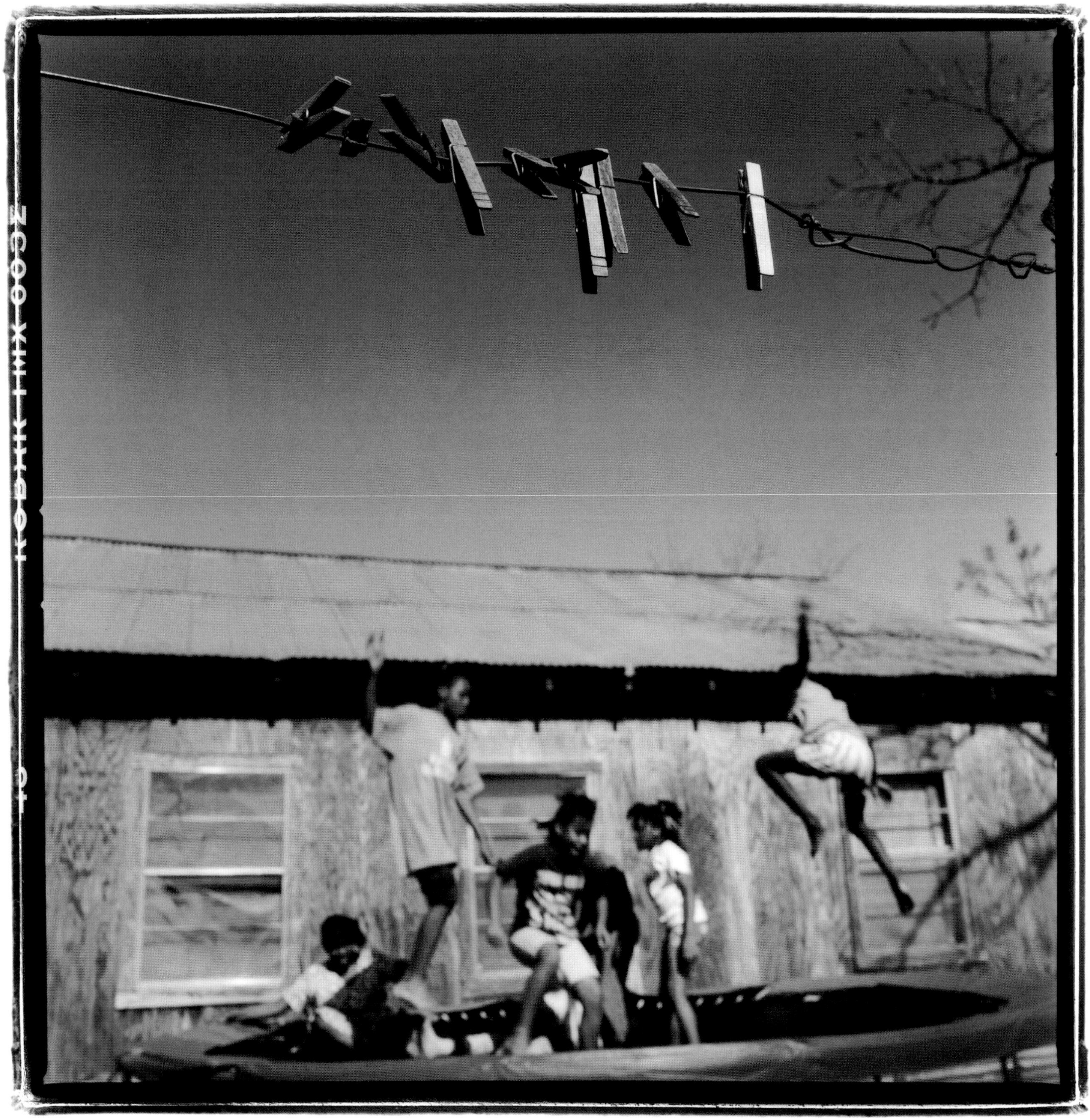

Clothespins

Stretching

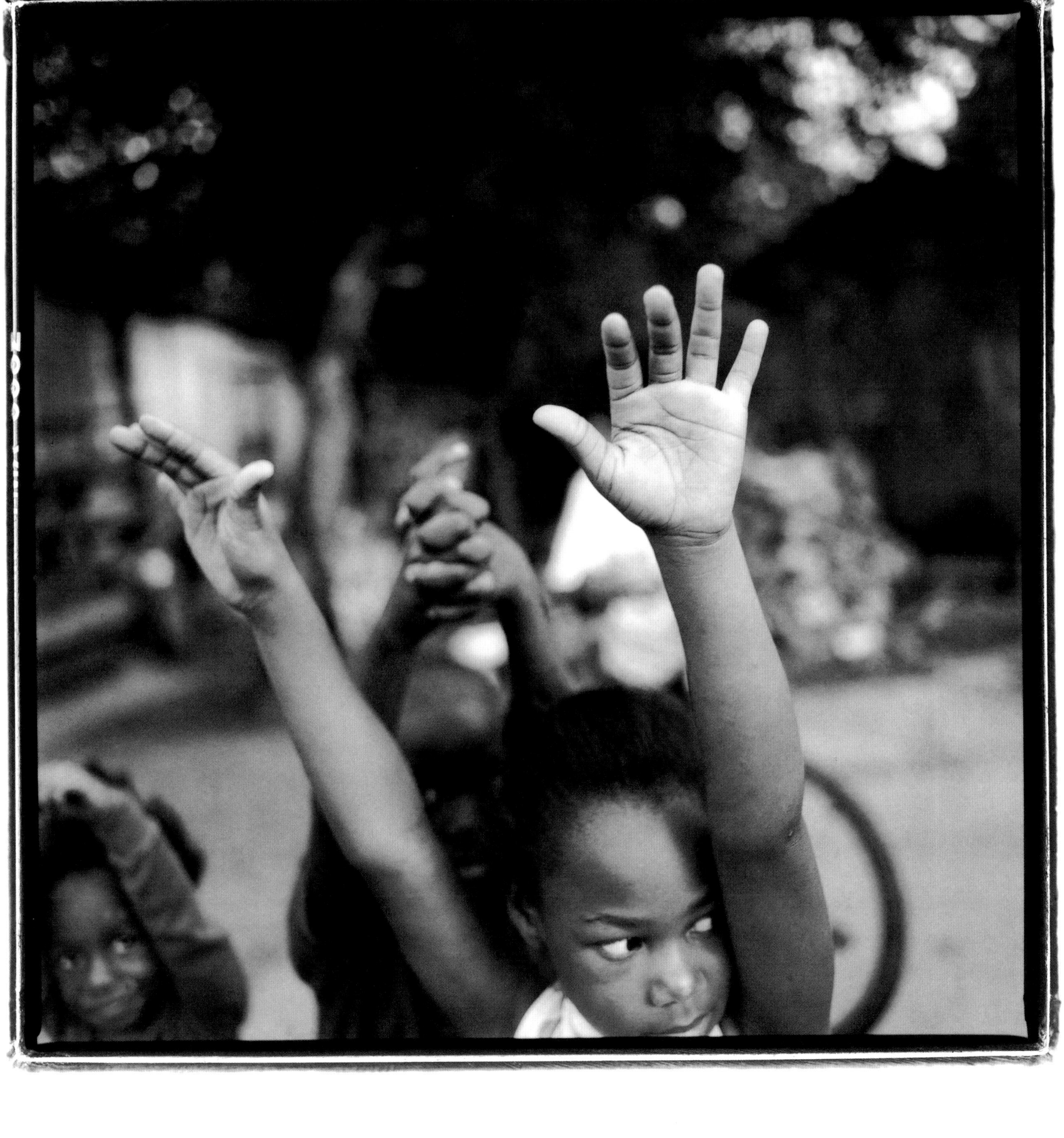

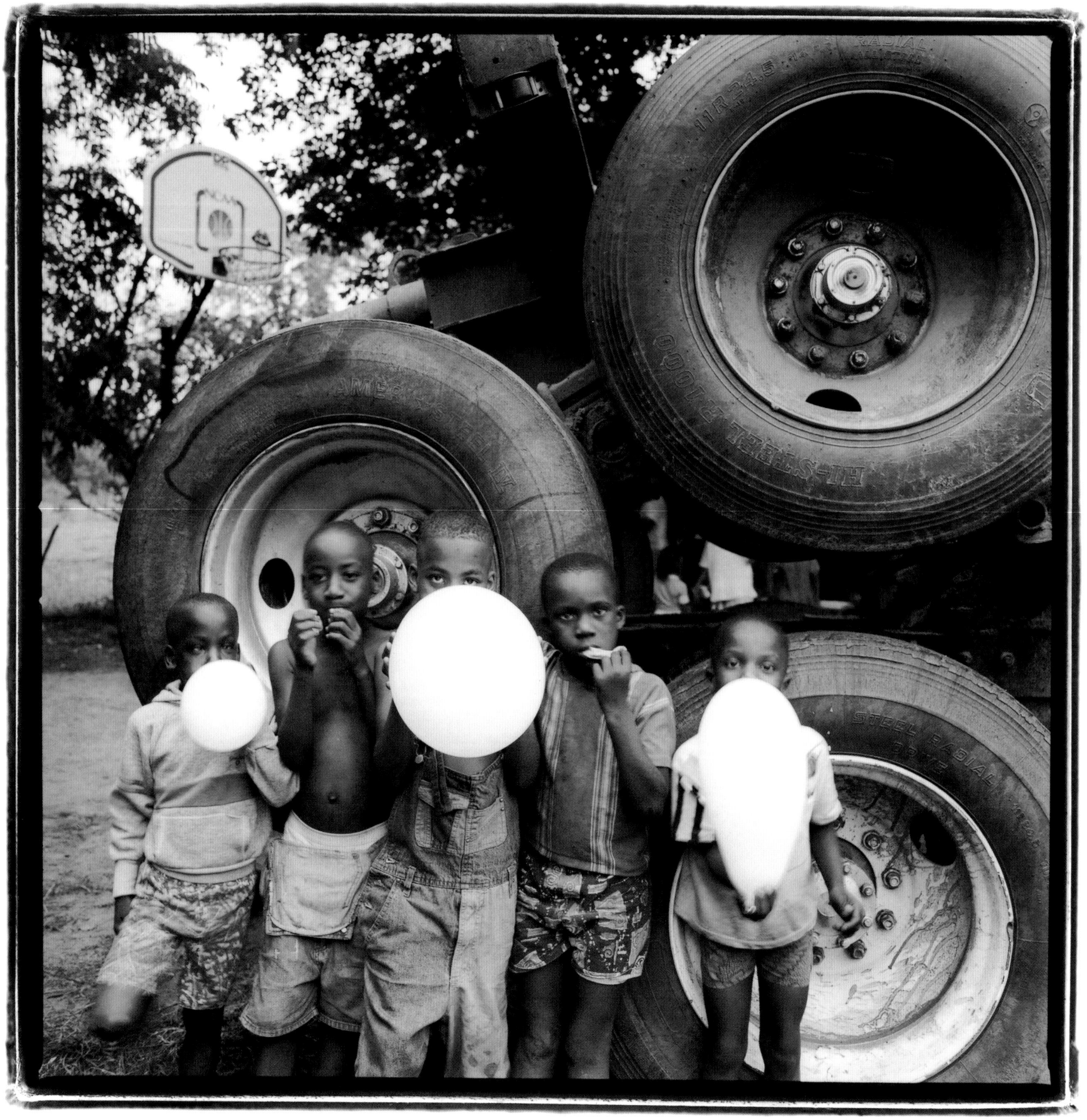
STEEL RADIAL

Balloons

Porch Horse

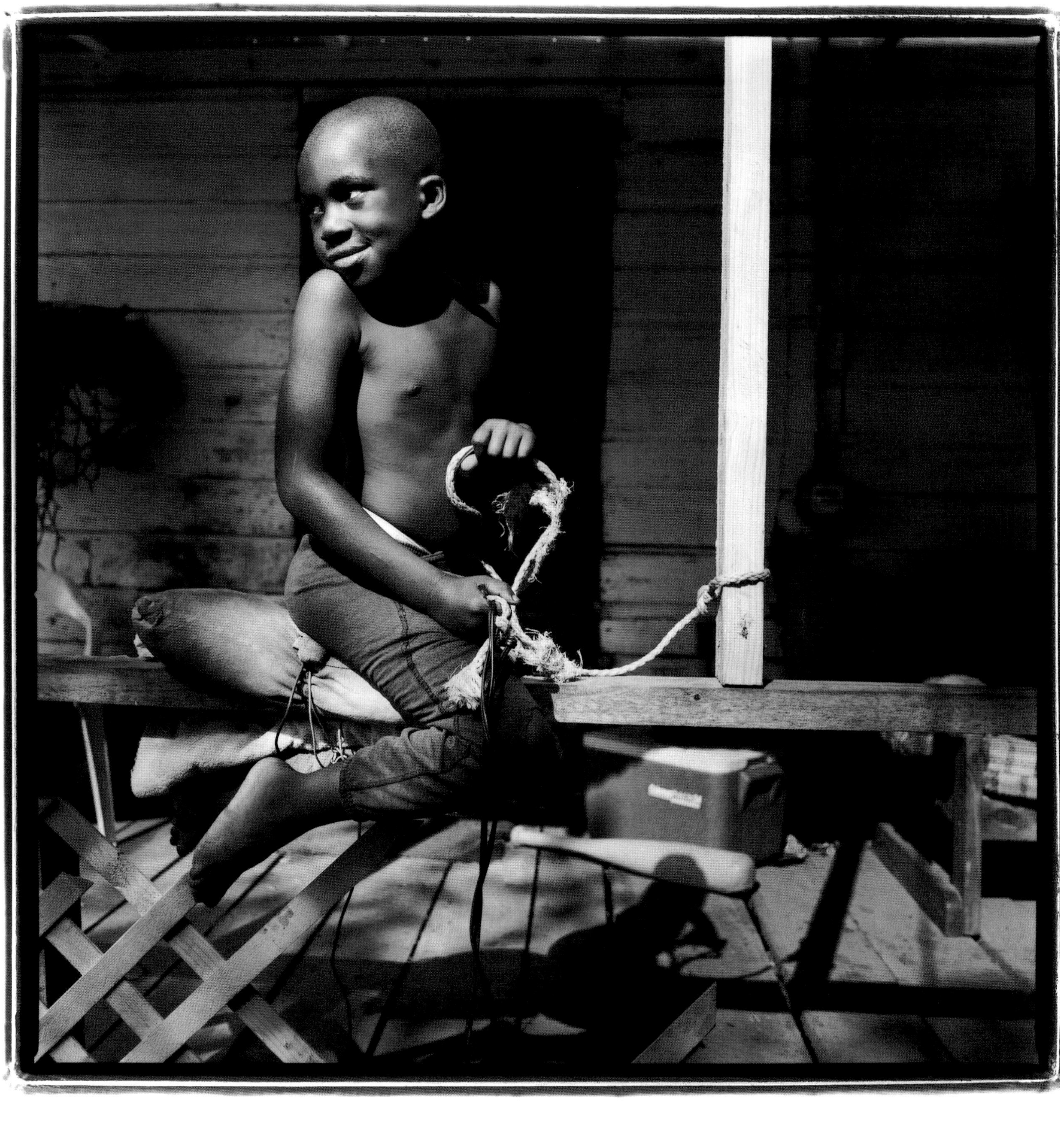

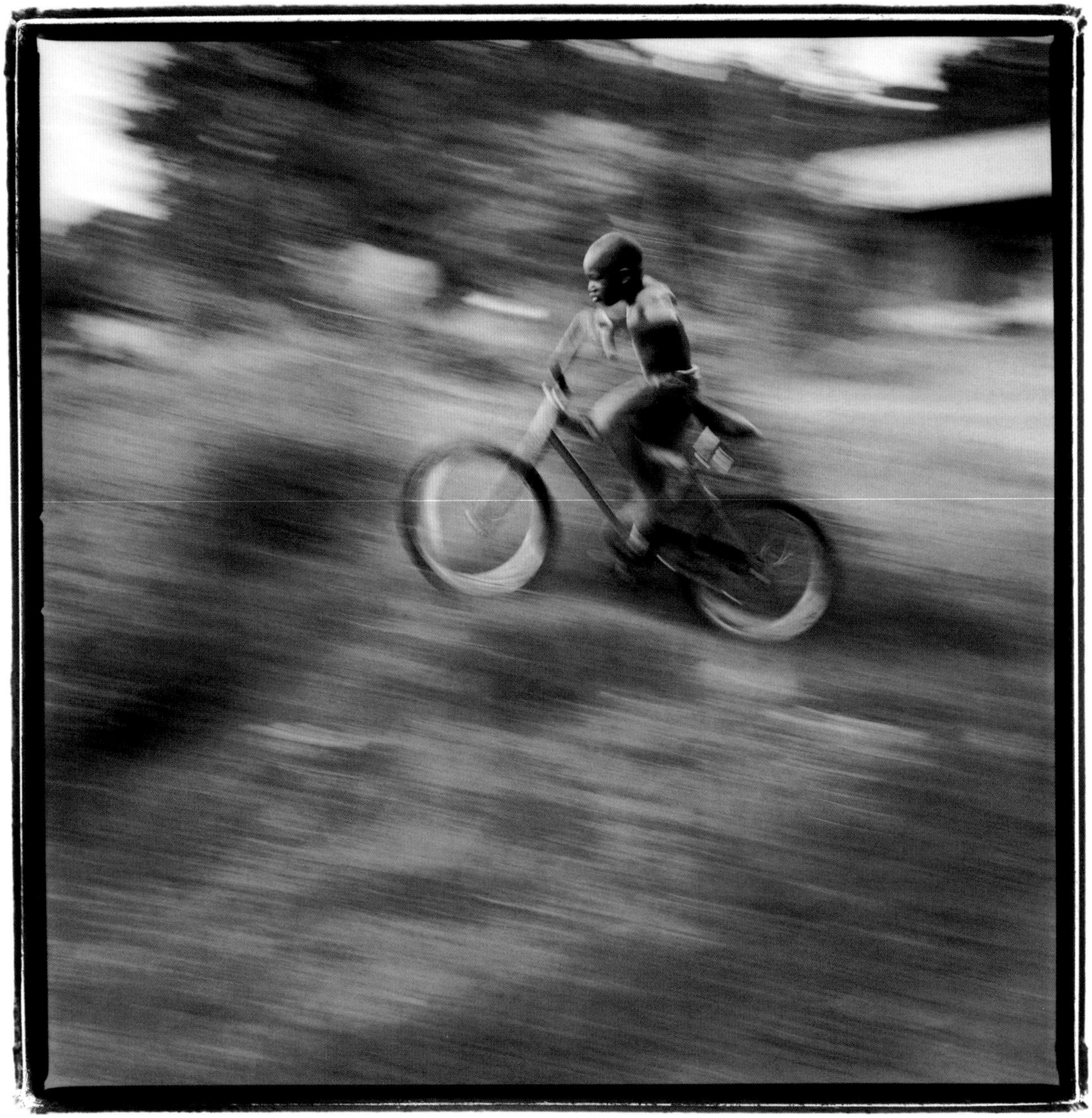

Bicycle Motion

Trey's Ride

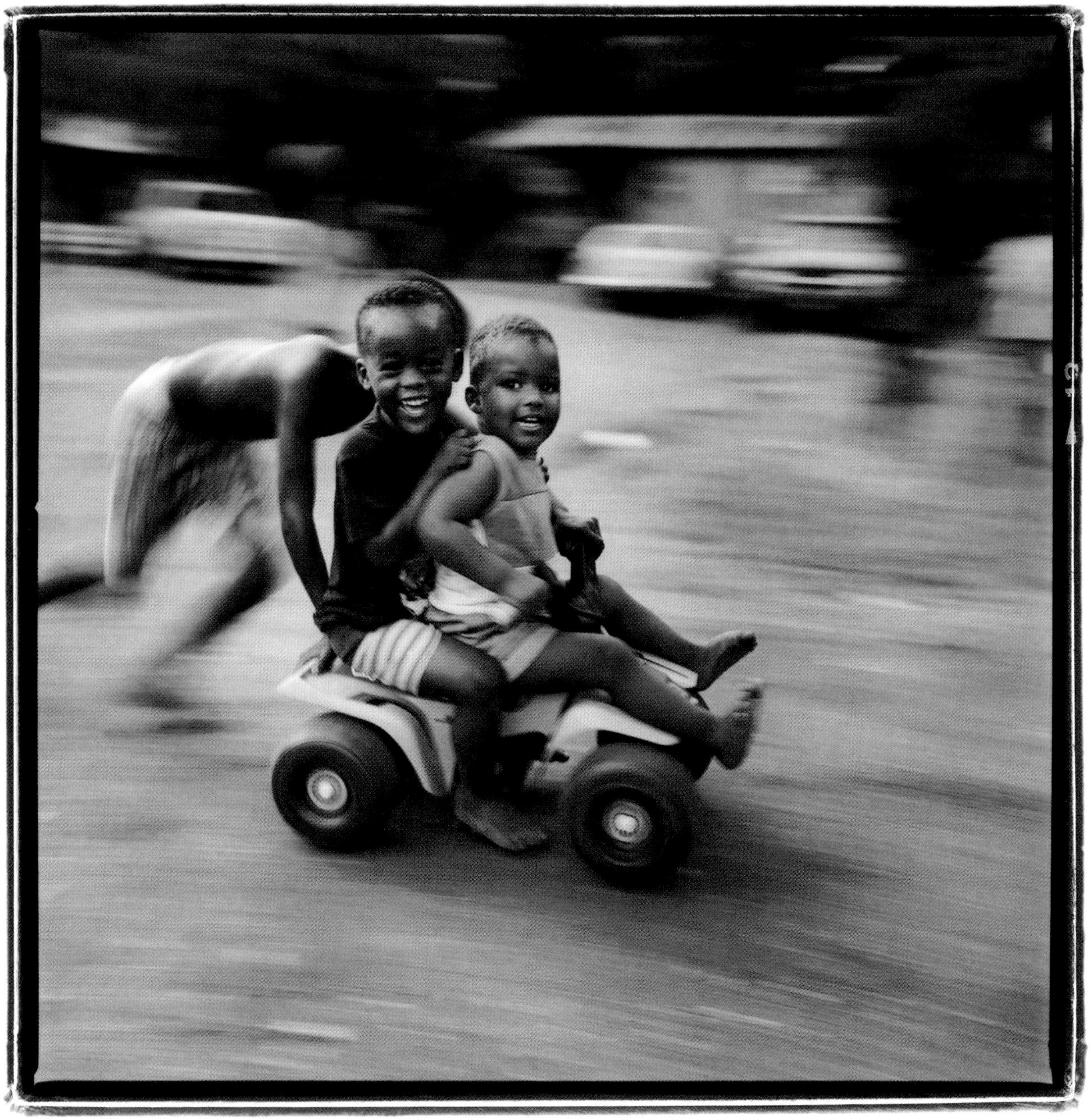

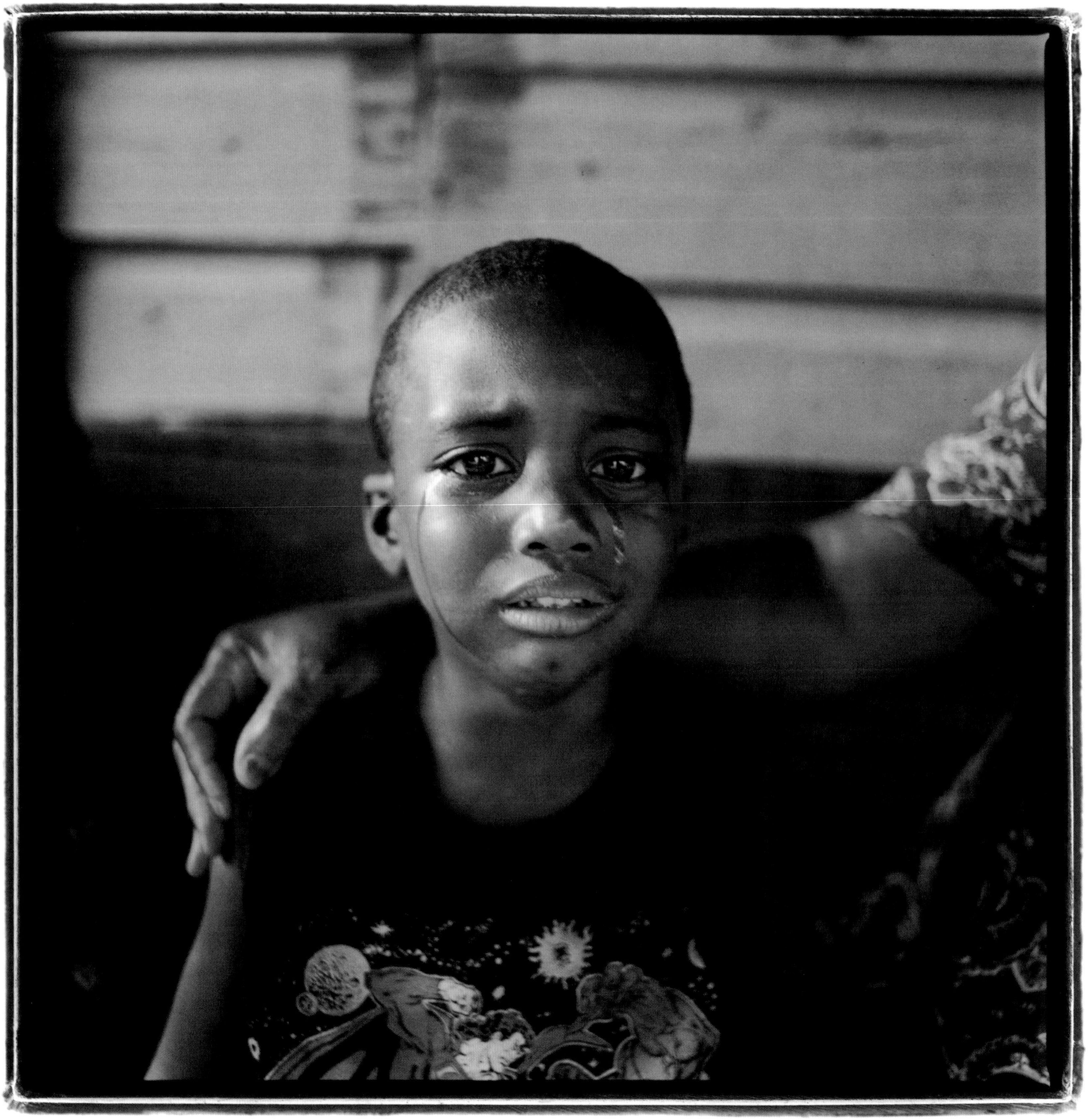

53

Tears

1, 2, 3, Red Light

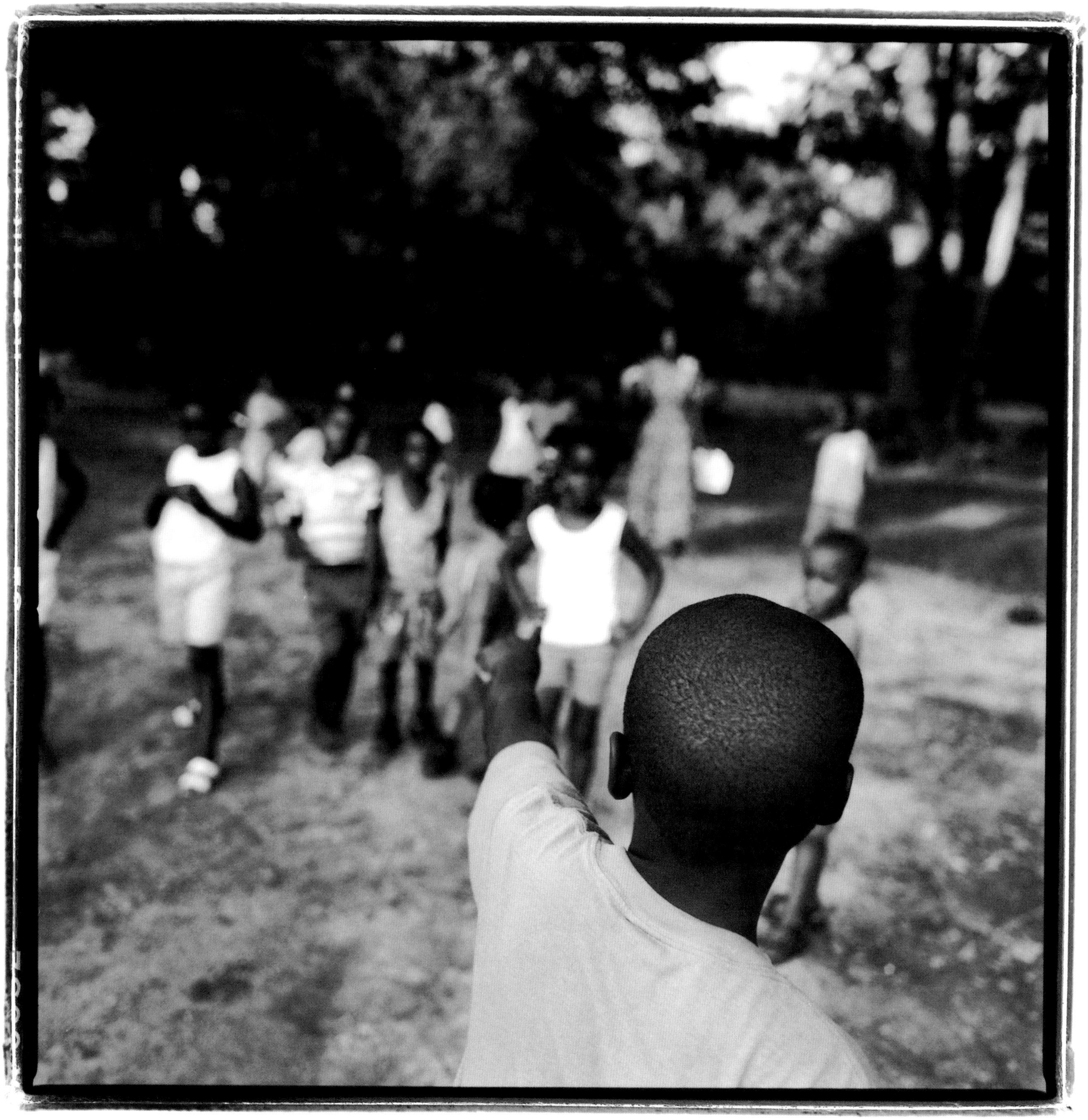

56

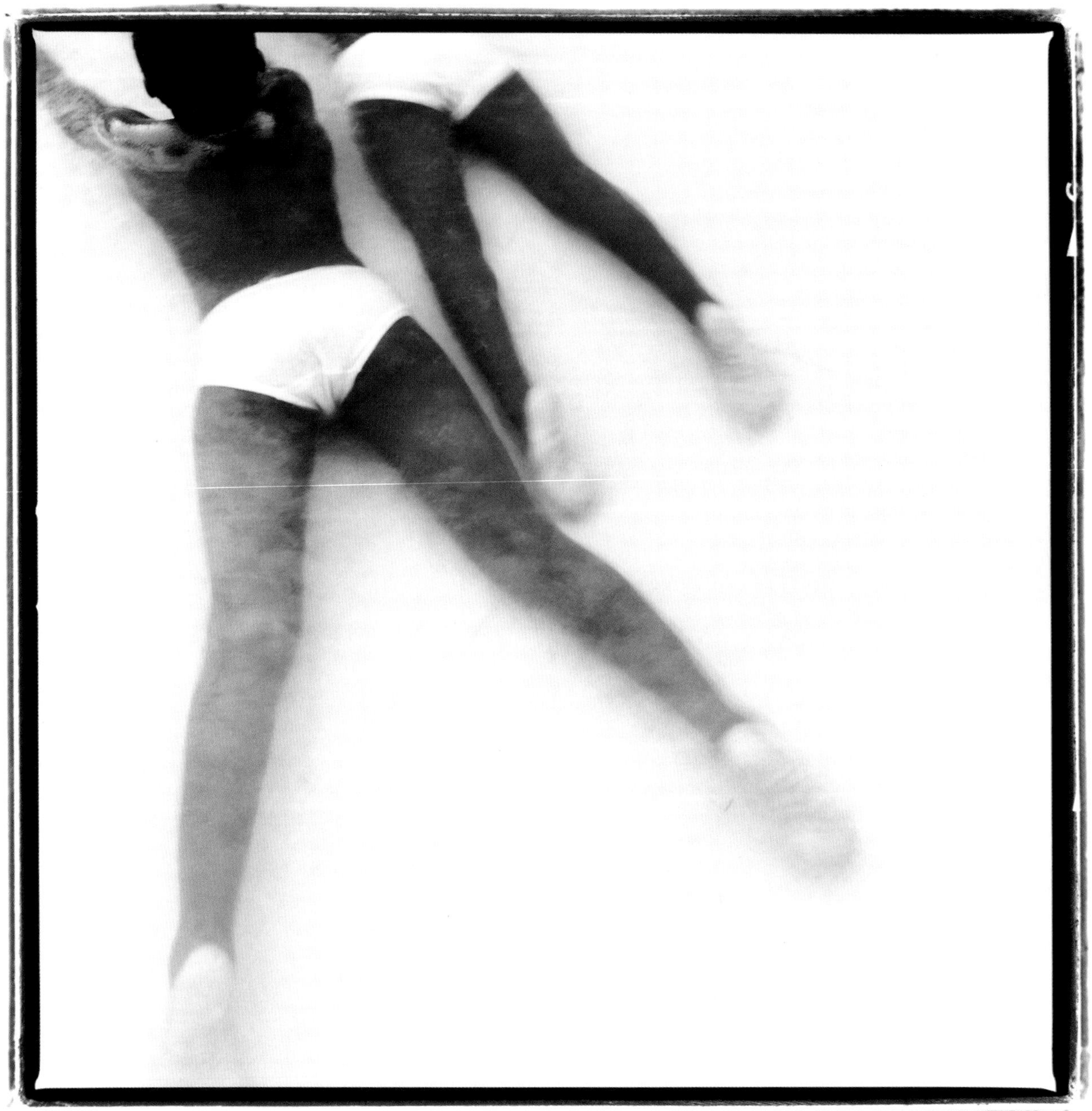

Swimmers

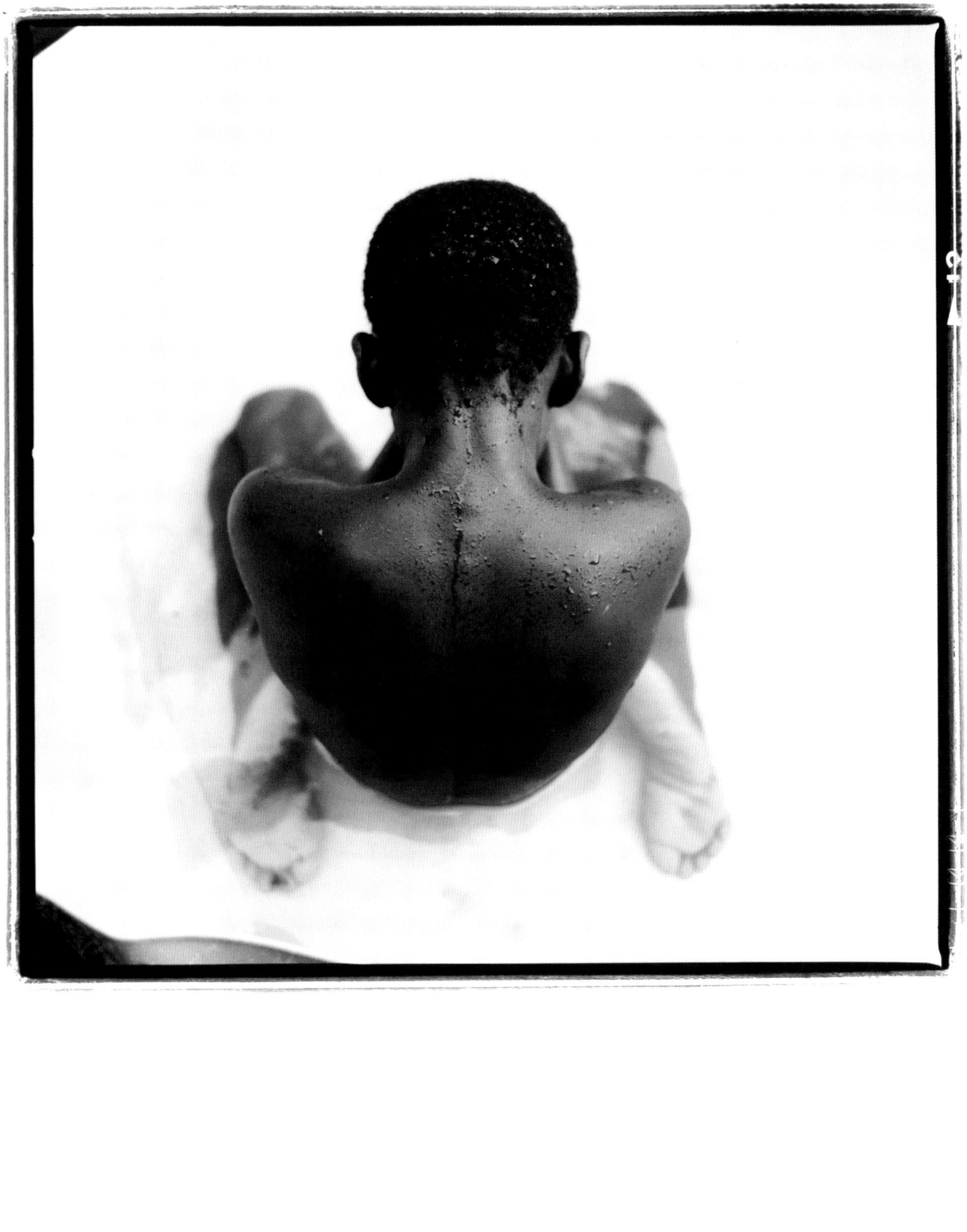

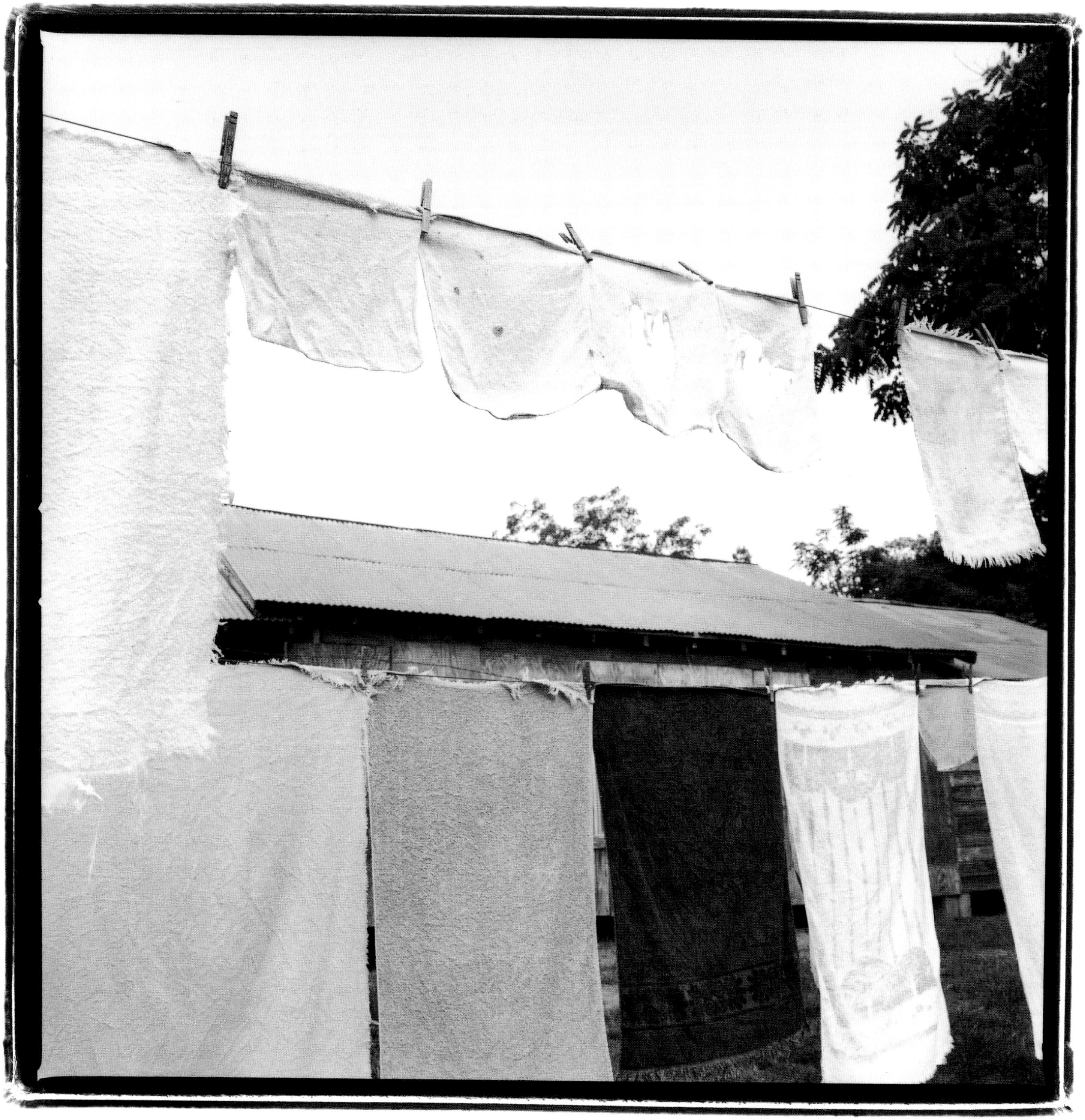

Heart Cloth

Sleeping Dog

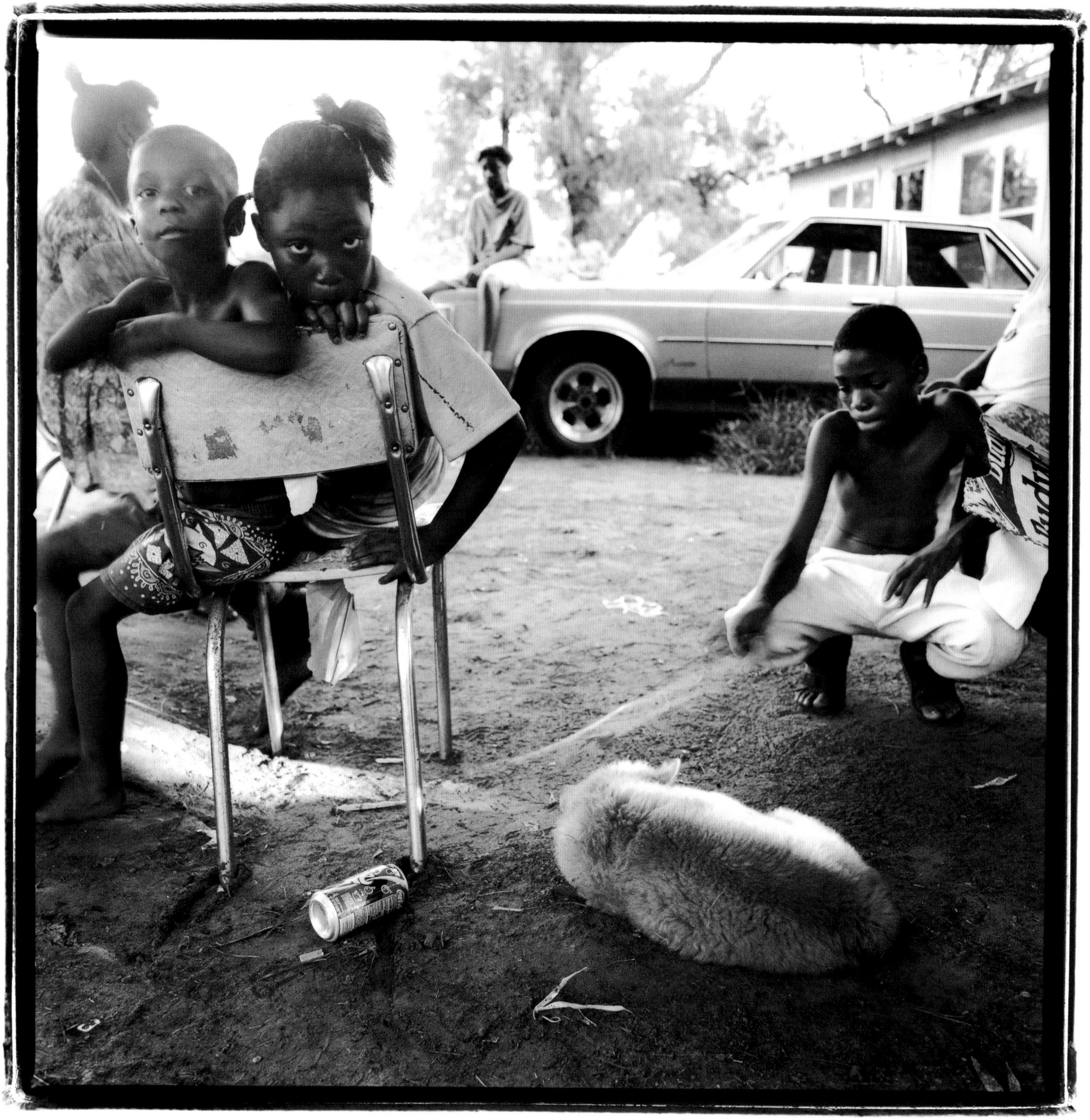

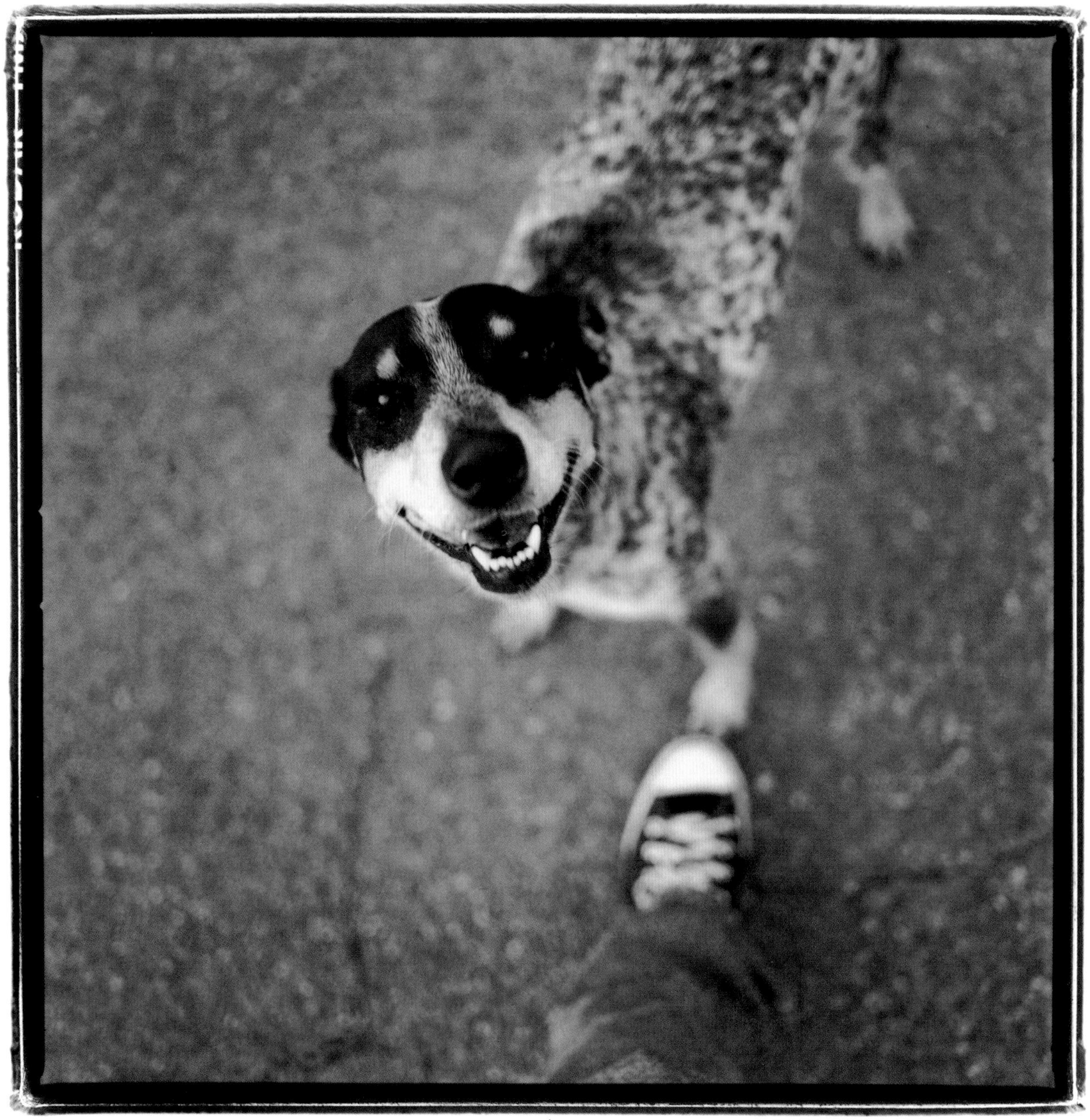

Speckled Dog

Black Dog

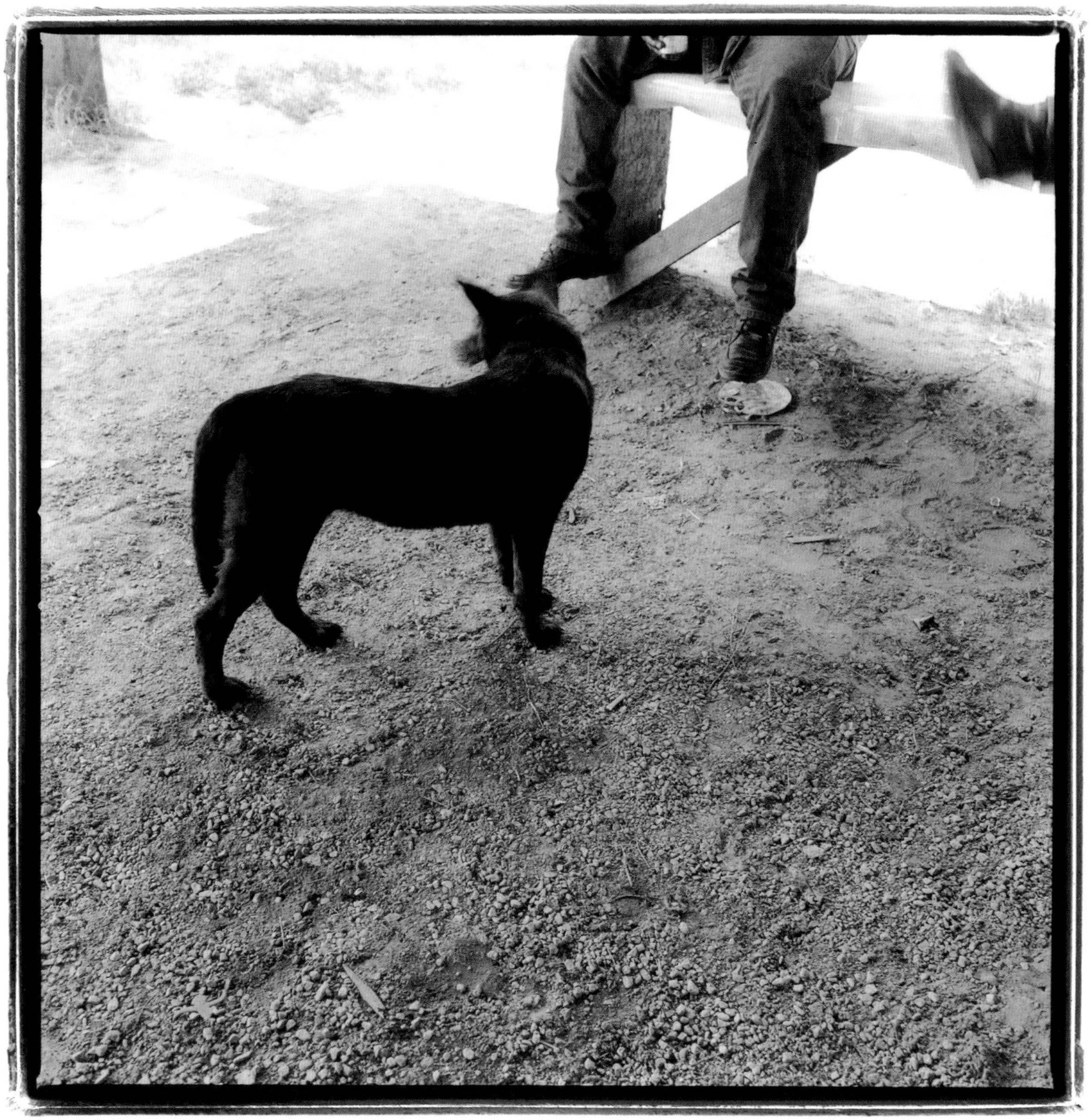

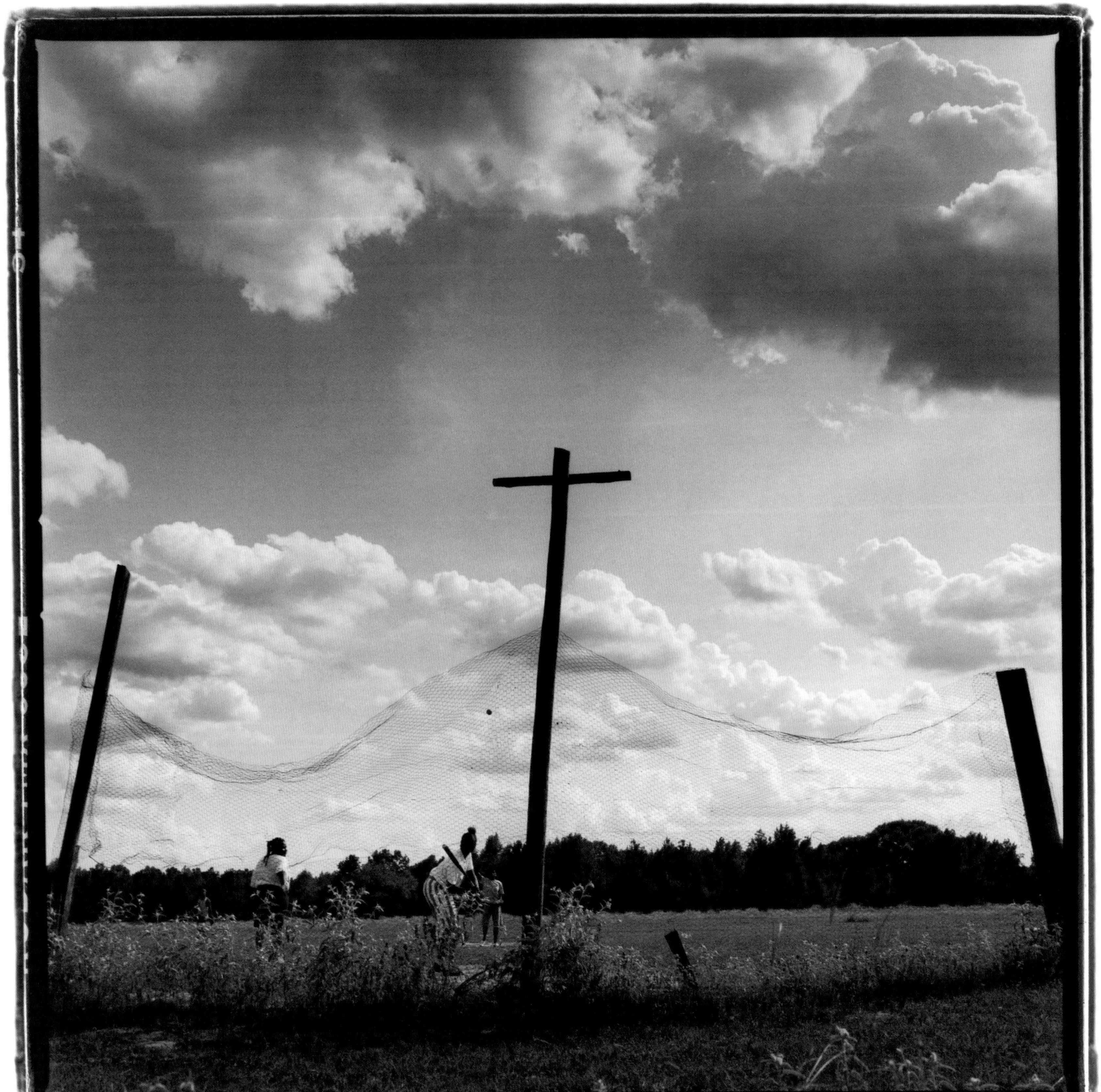

Softball

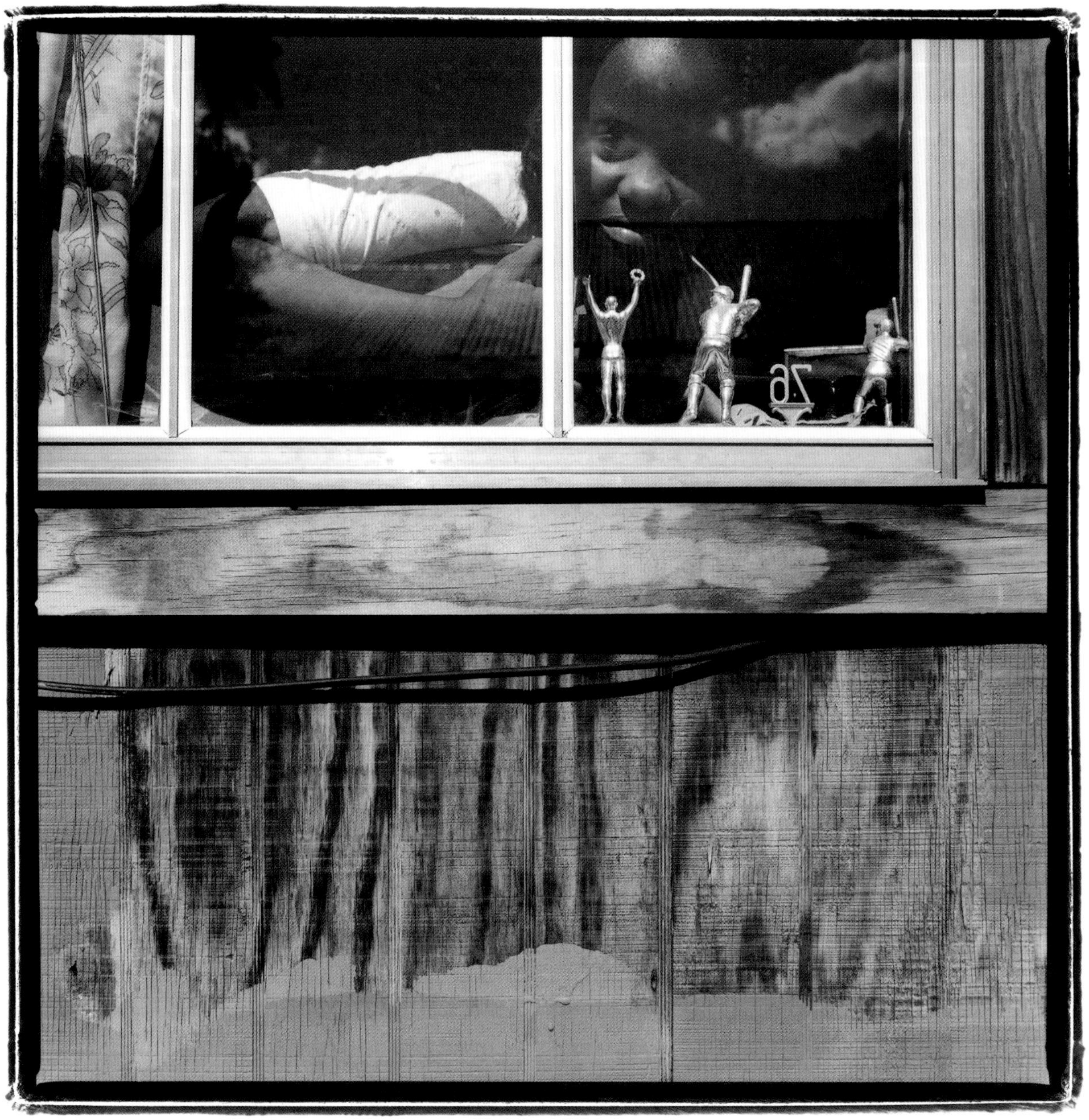

Trophy Window

Trophy Room

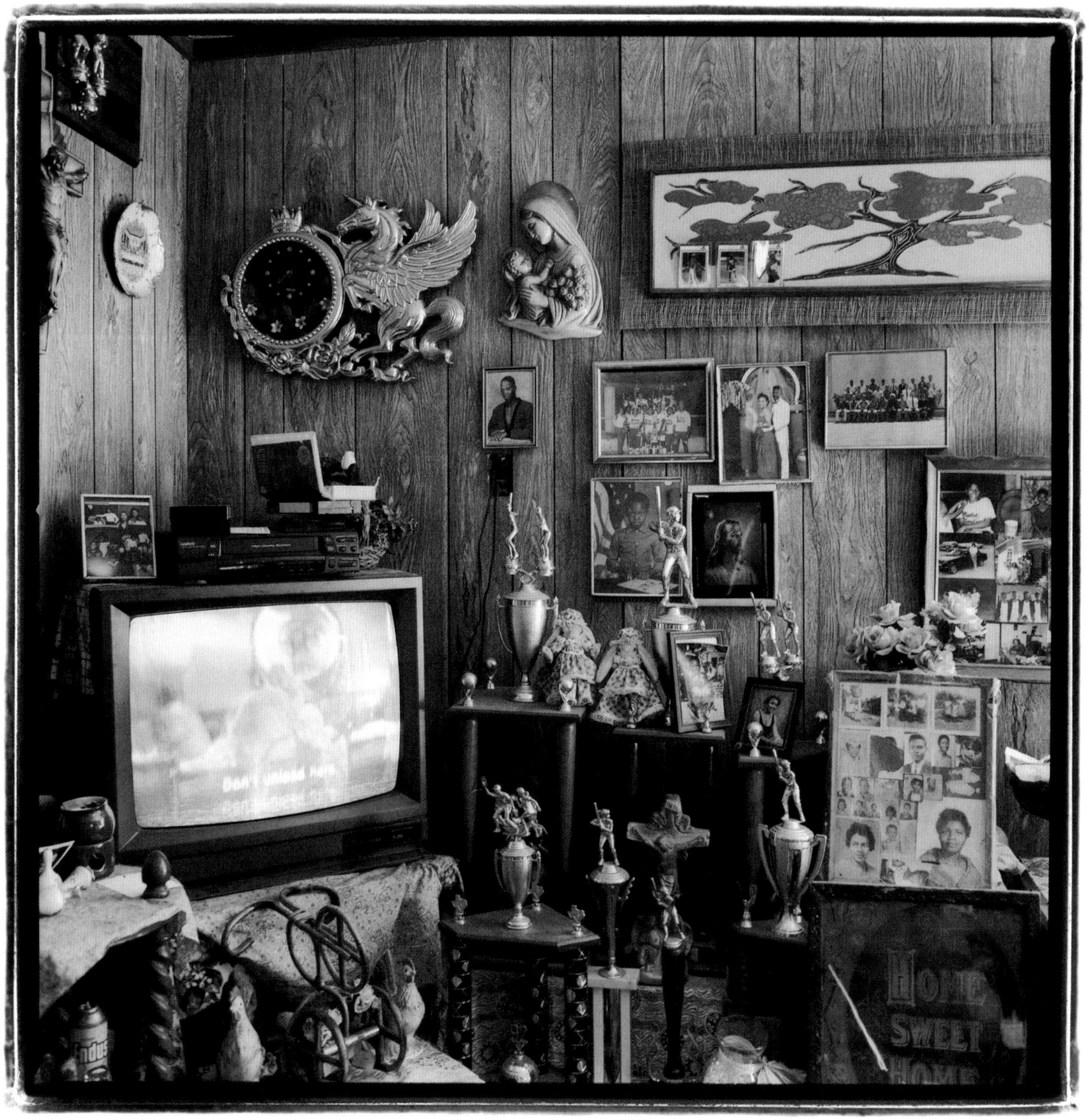

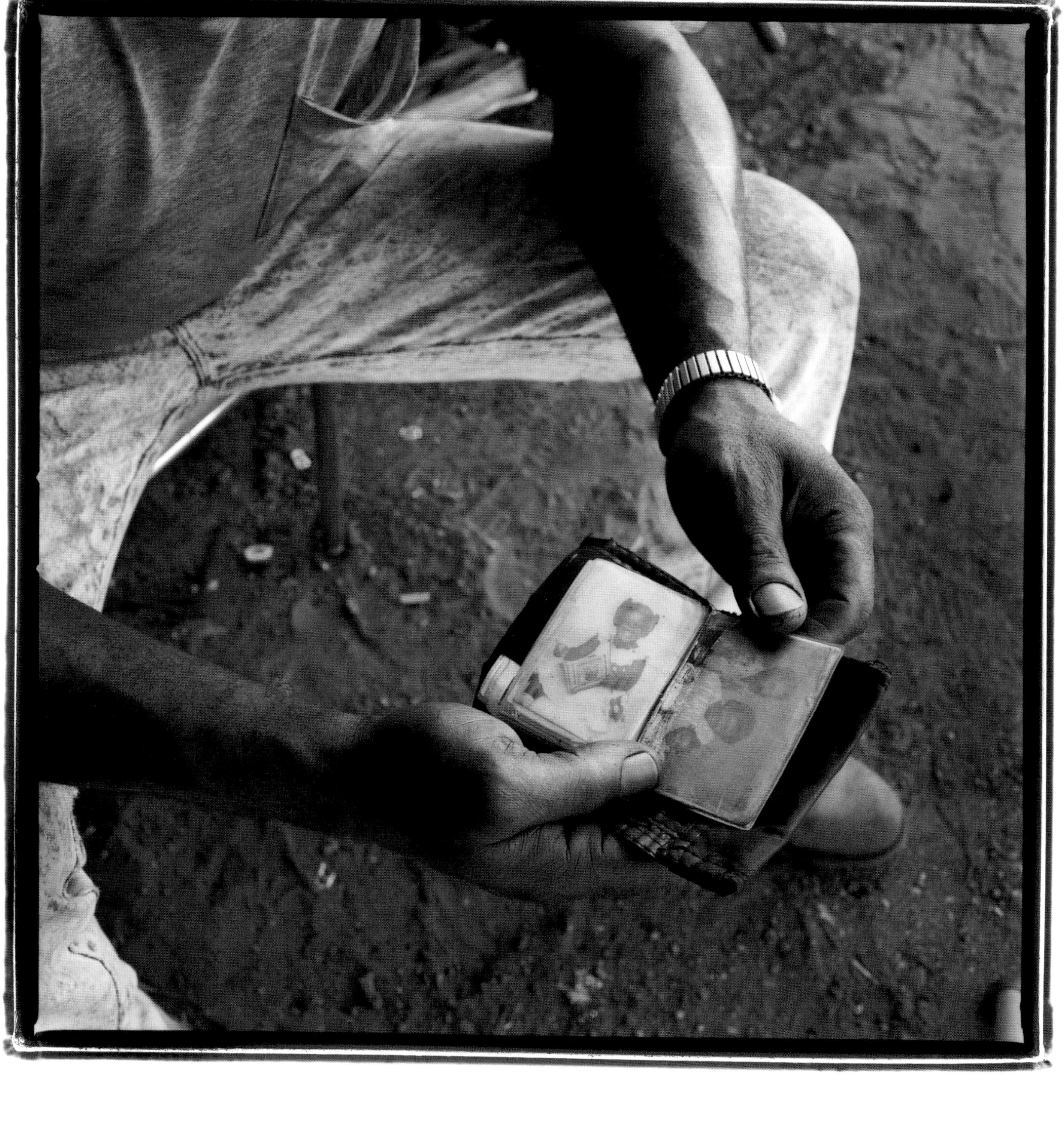

Cherry's Wallet

Memories

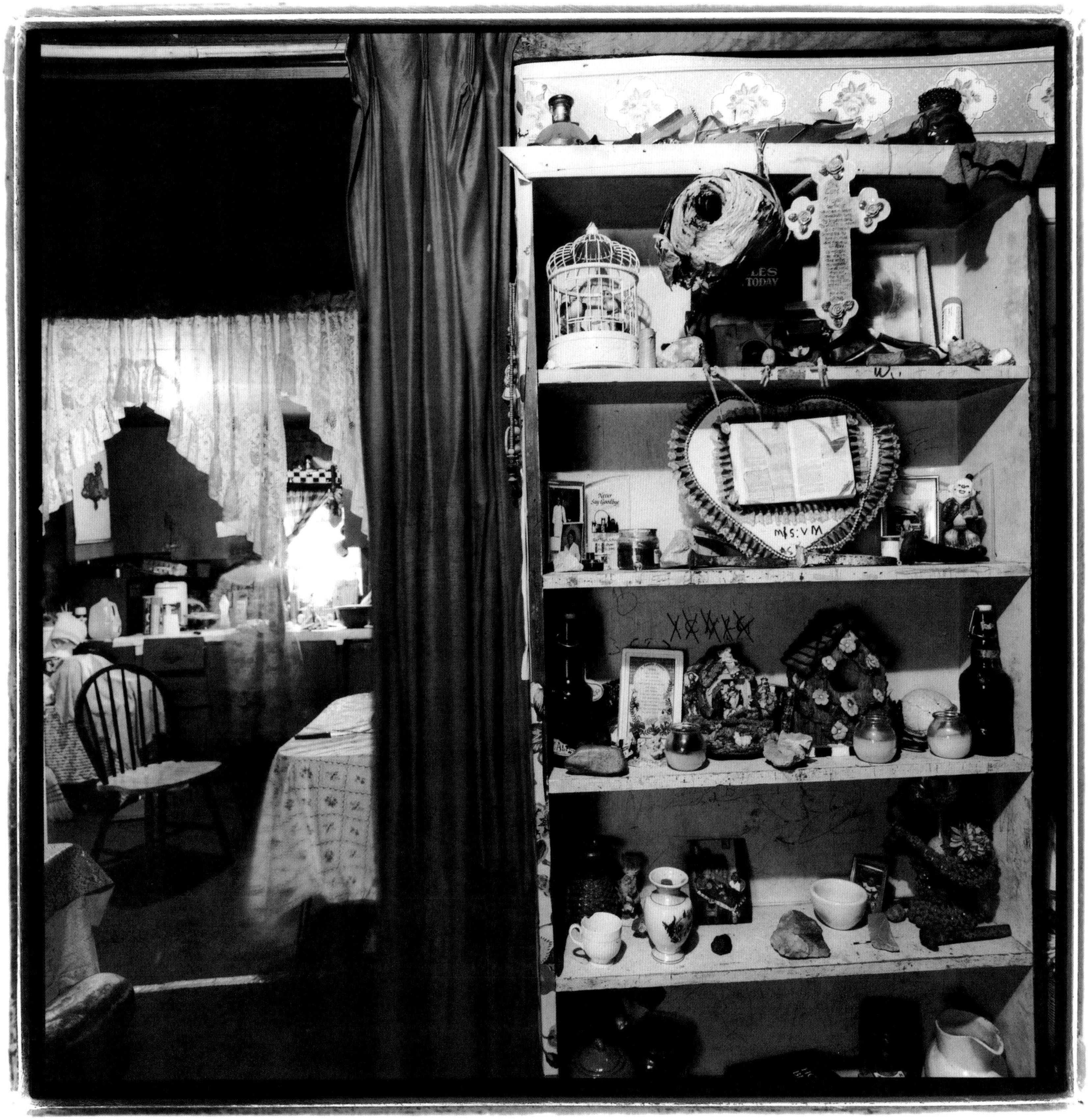
Never Say Goodbye

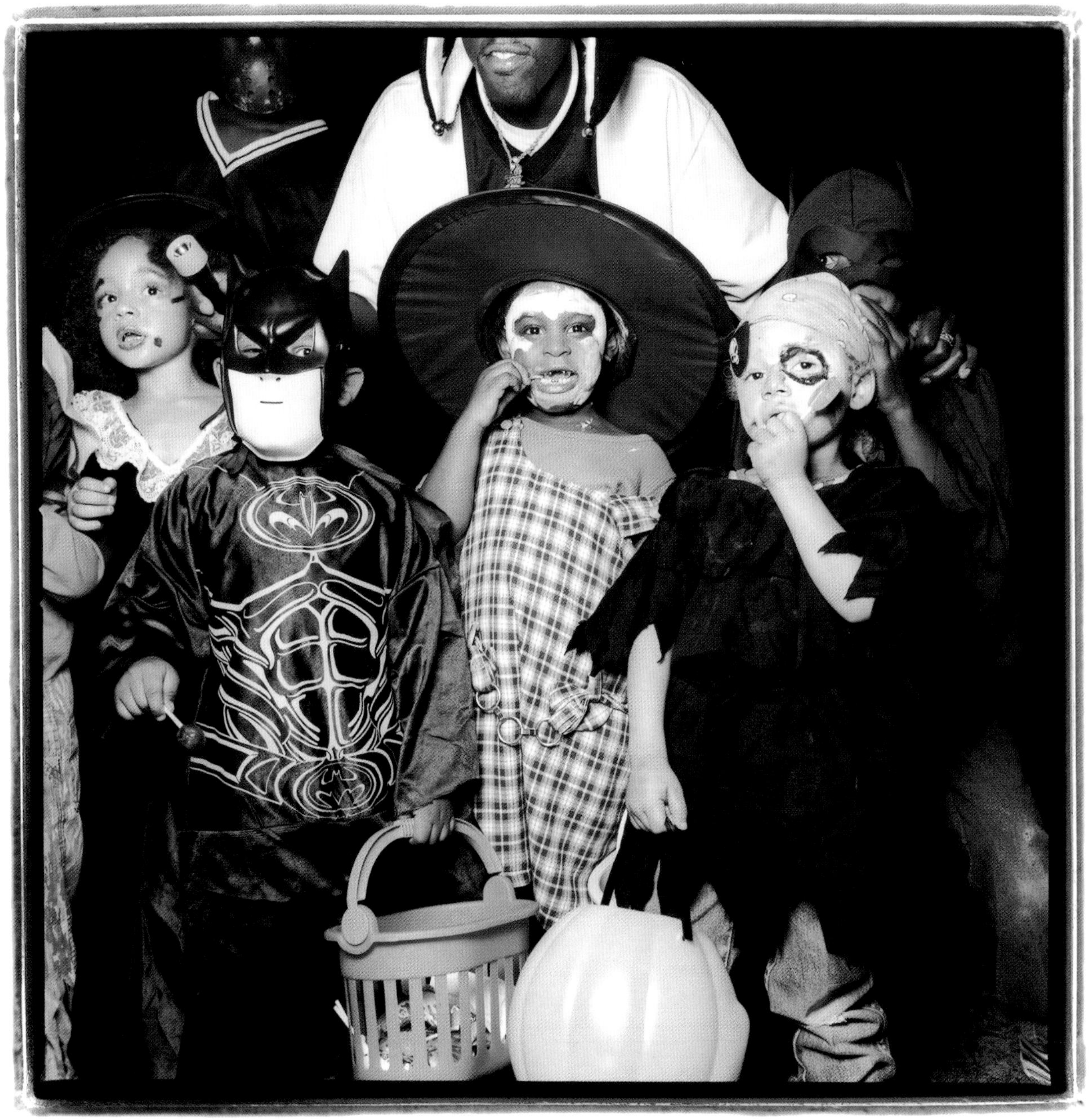

Trick or Treat

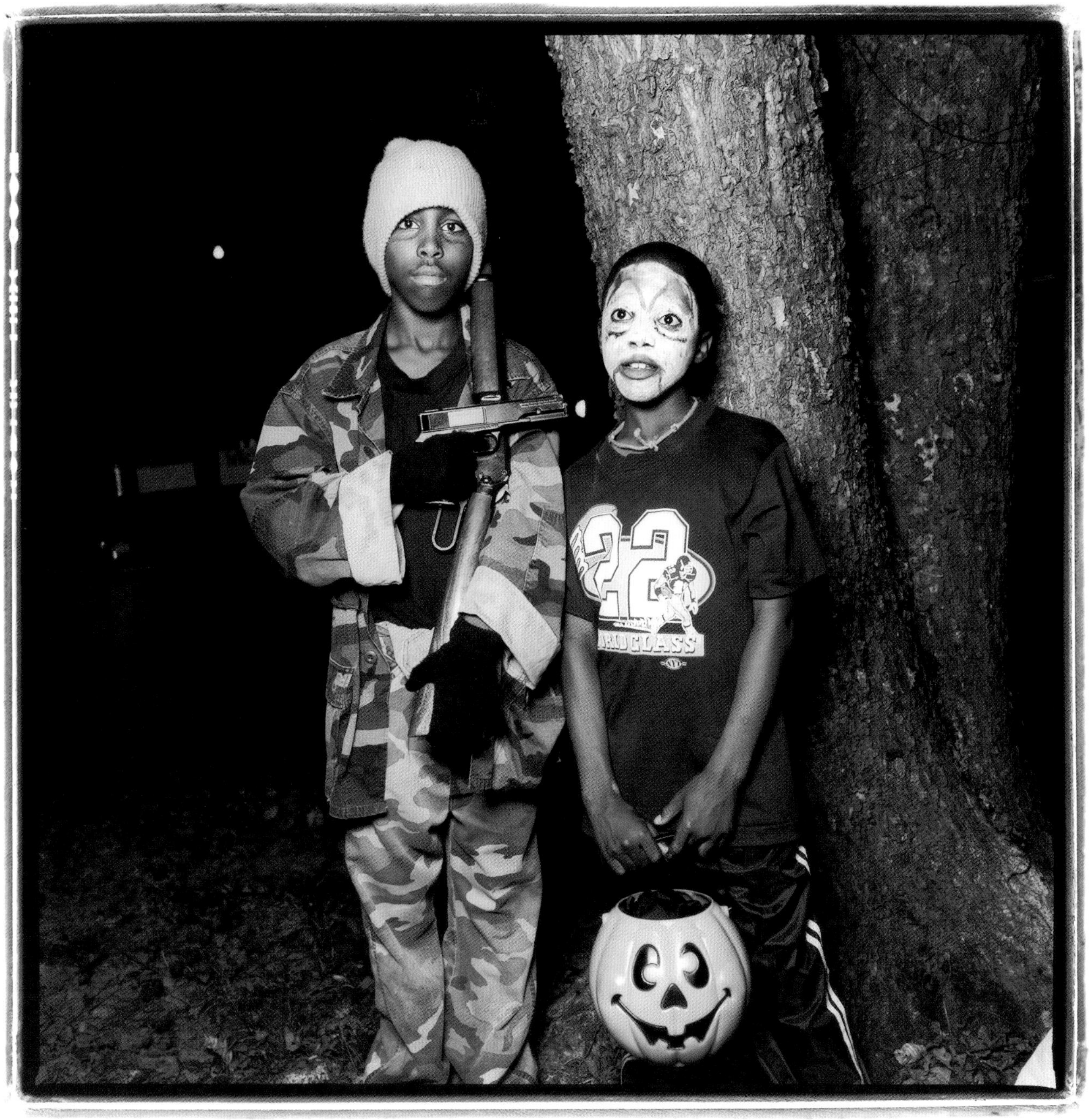
22
HARDCLASS

74

The Last Supper

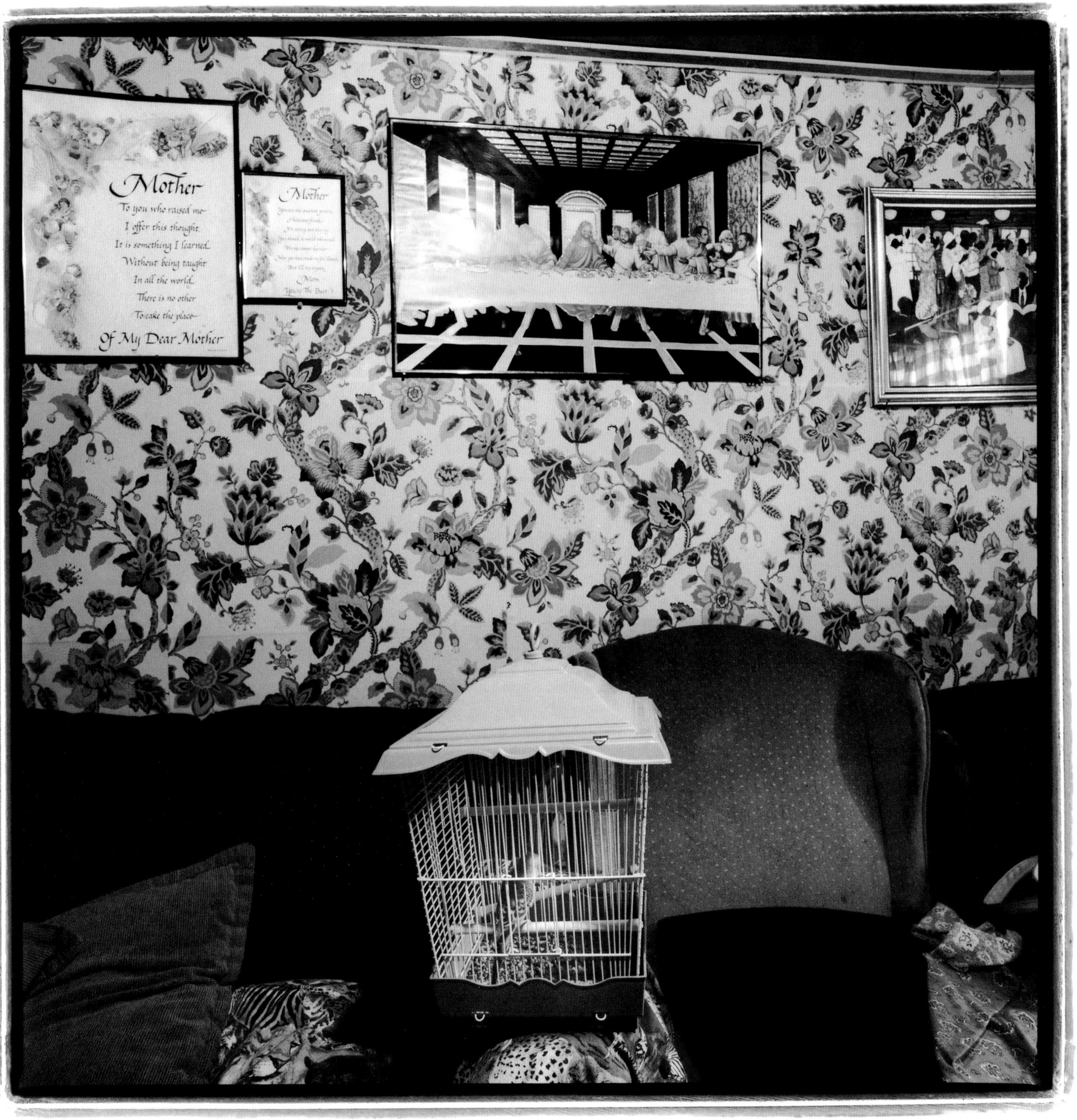
Mother
To you who raised me
I offer this thought
It is something I learned
Without being taught
In all the world
There is no other
To take the place
Of My Dear Mother

Without a Father

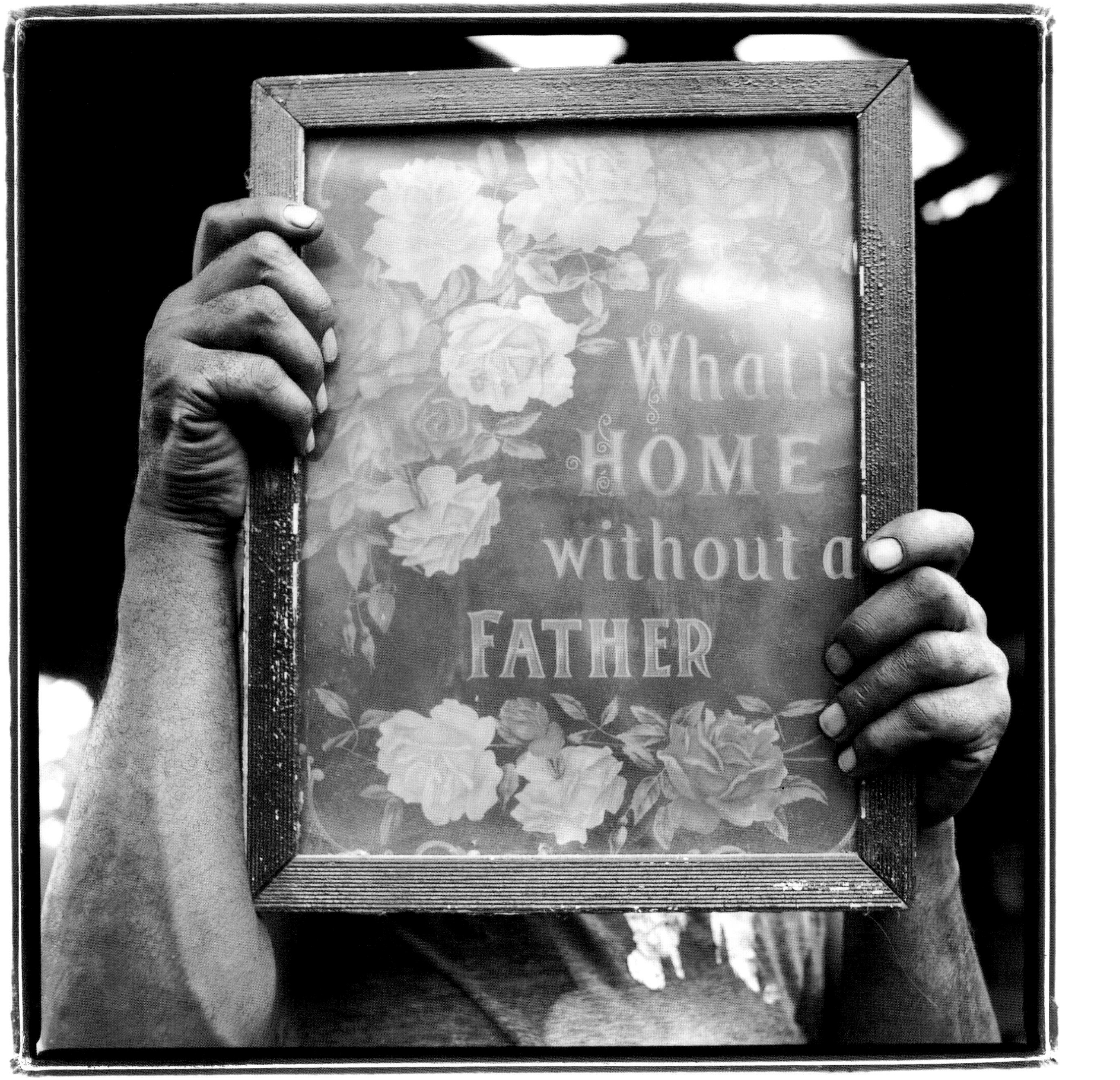
What is
HOME
without a
FATHER

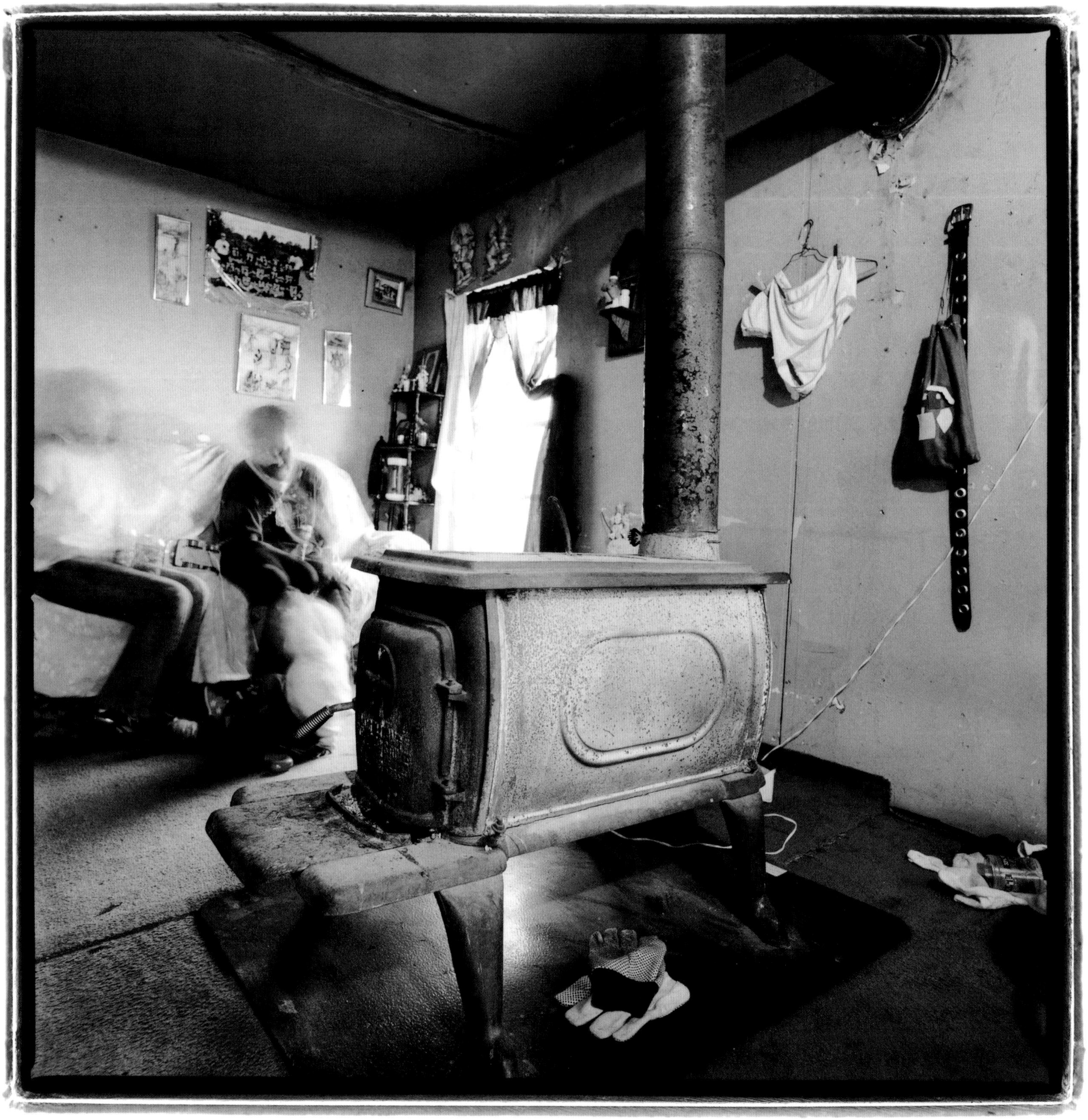

Winter Stove

Christmas Bicycle

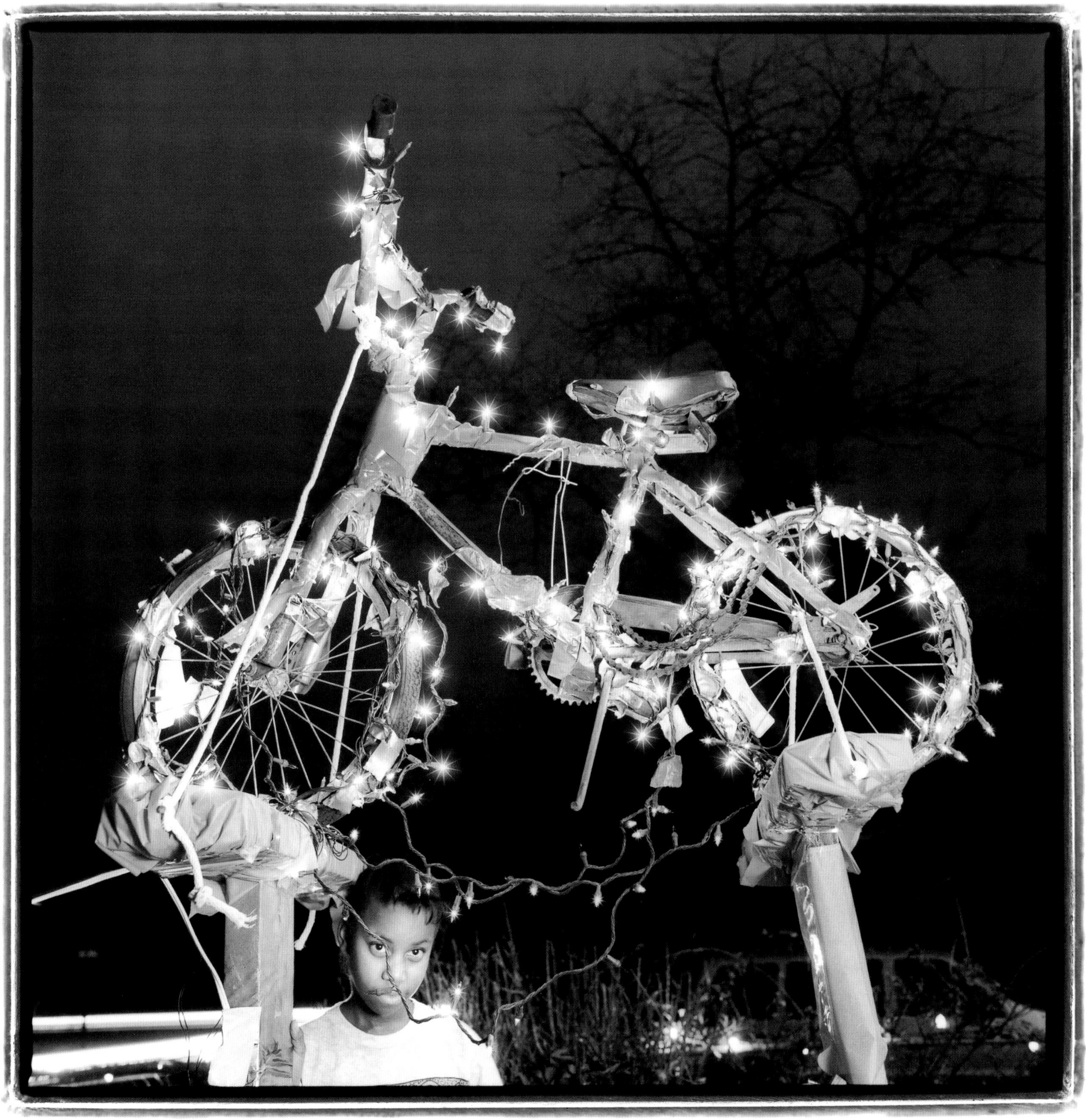

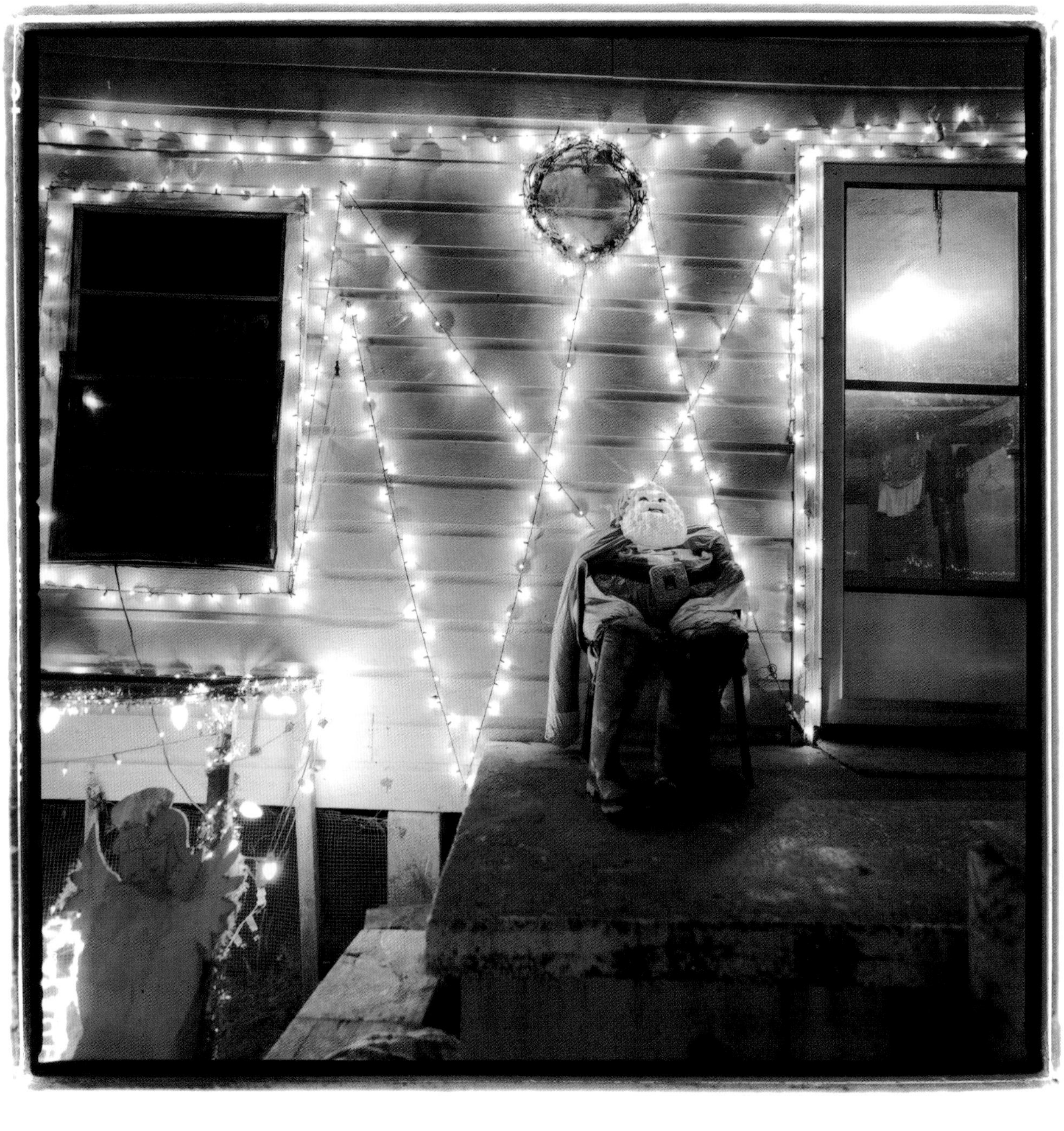

Christmas Lights

Christmas Lights

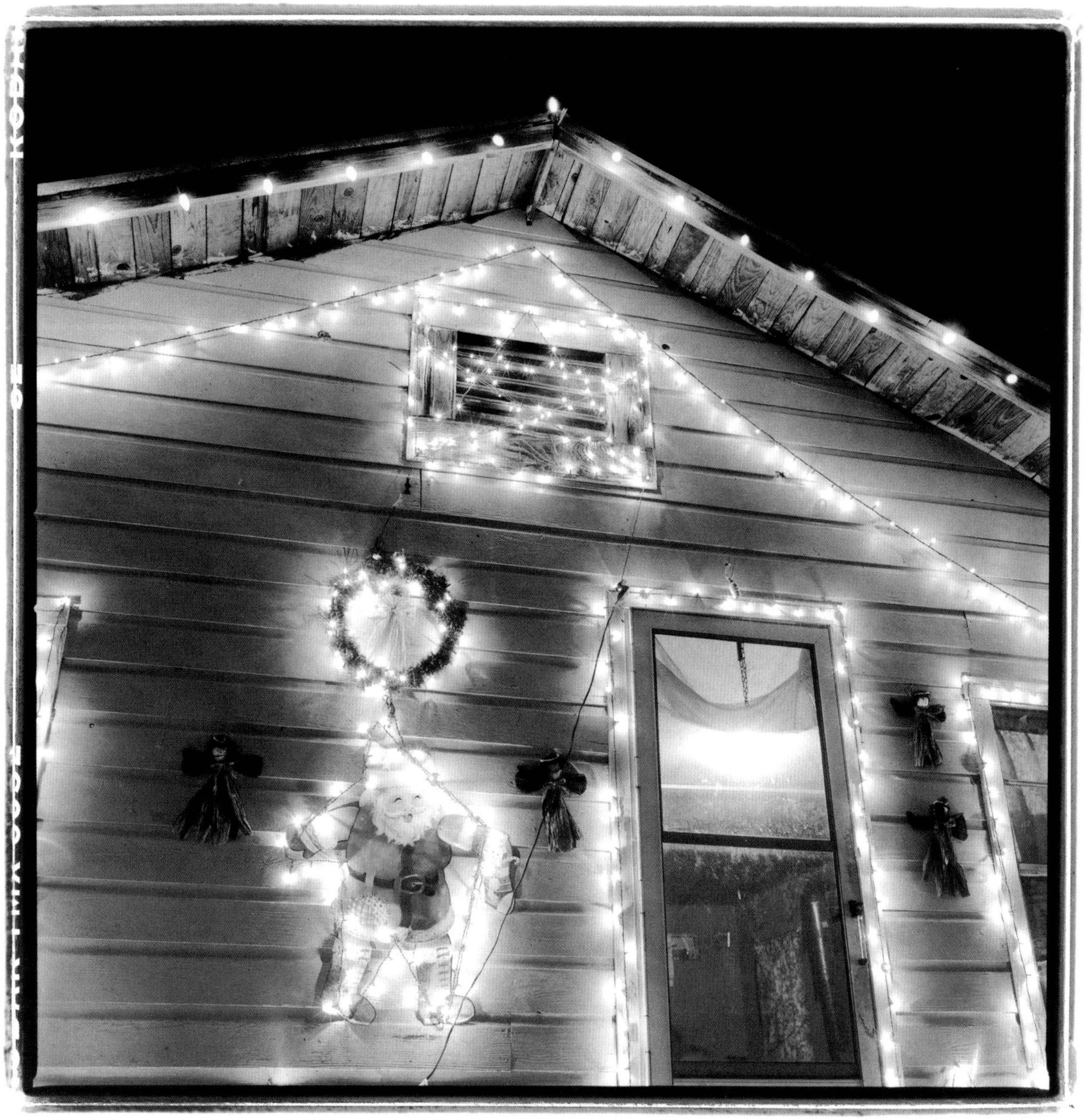

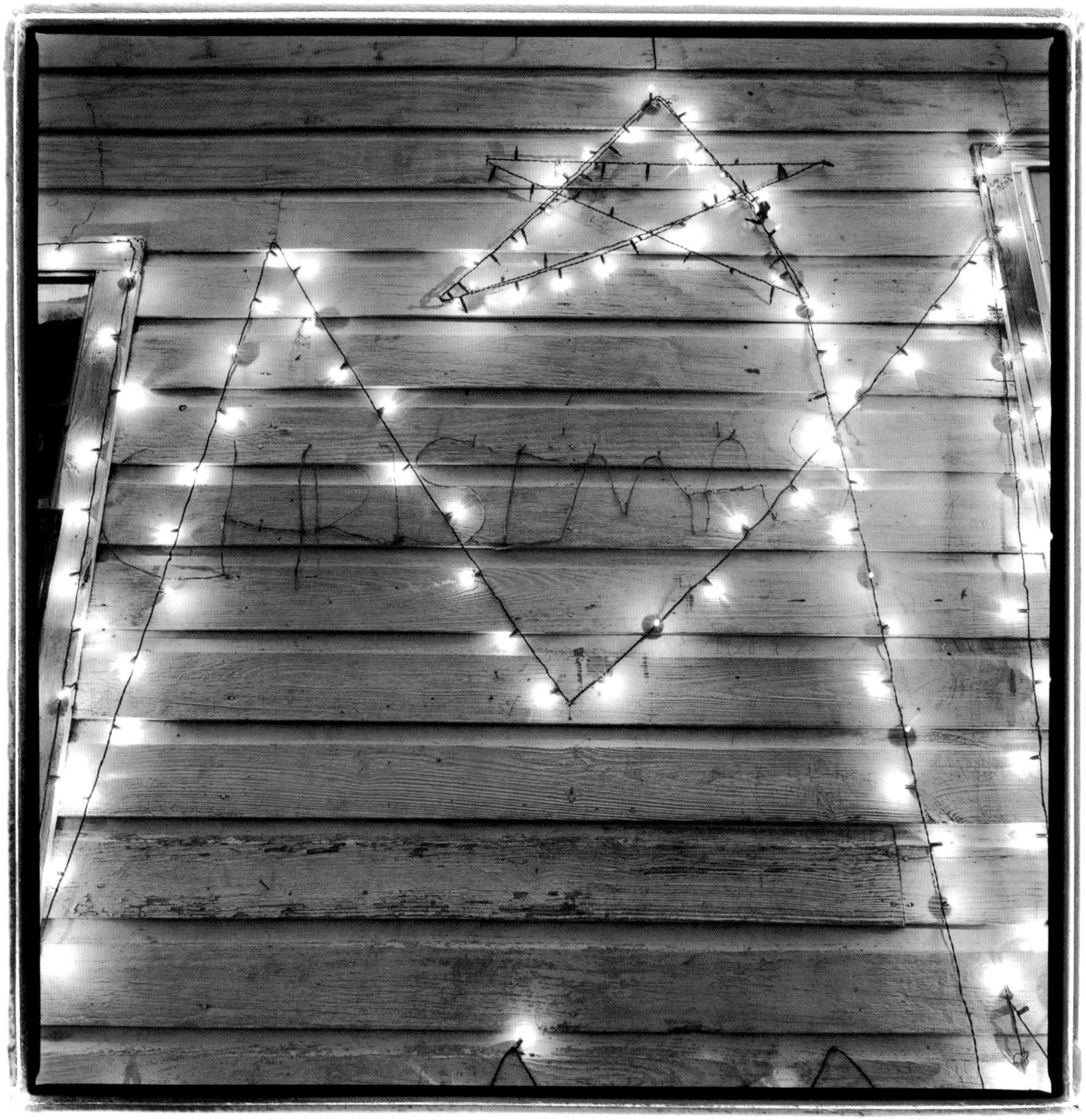

Christmas Lights

Christmas Lights

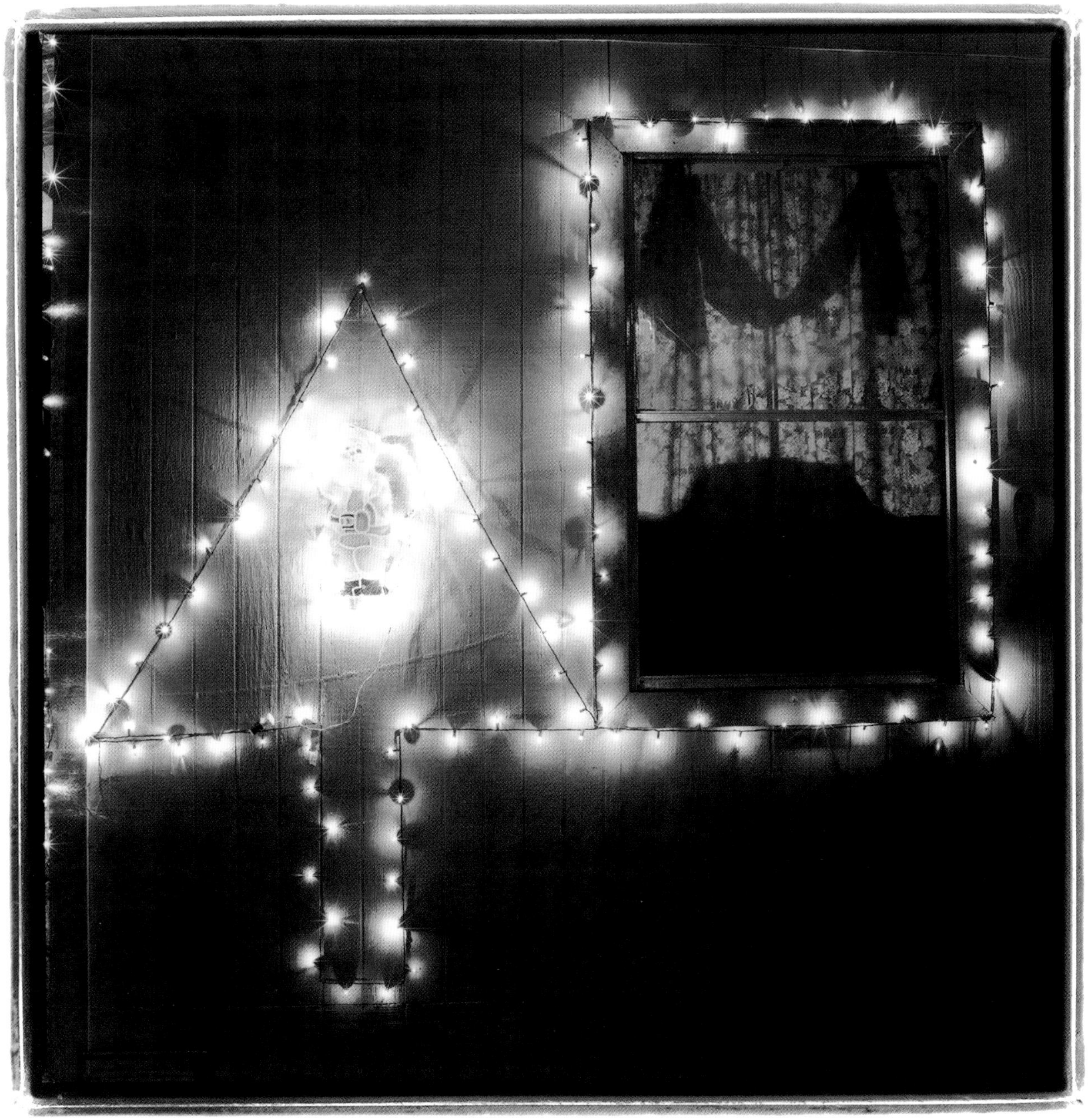

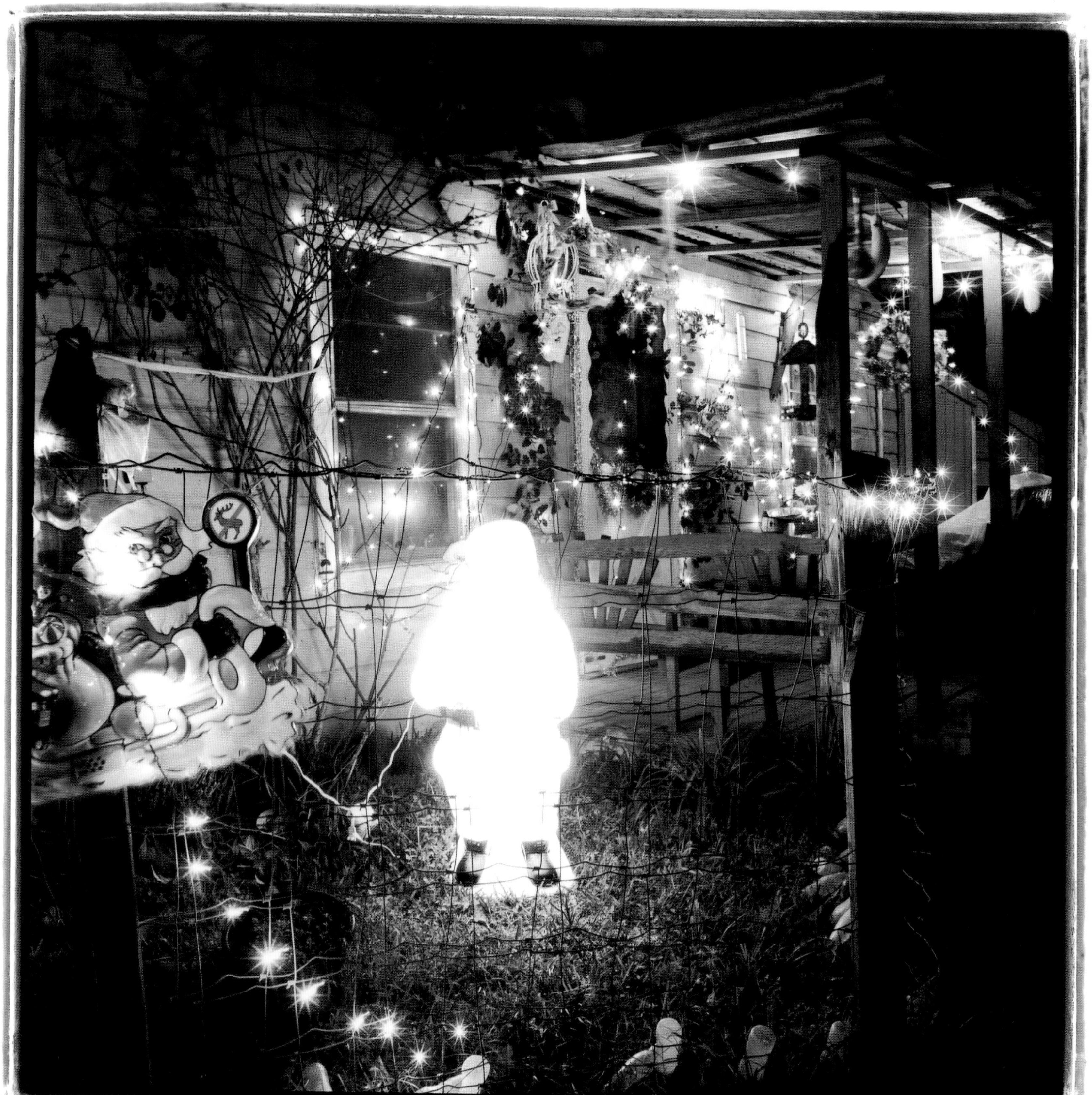

87

White Santa

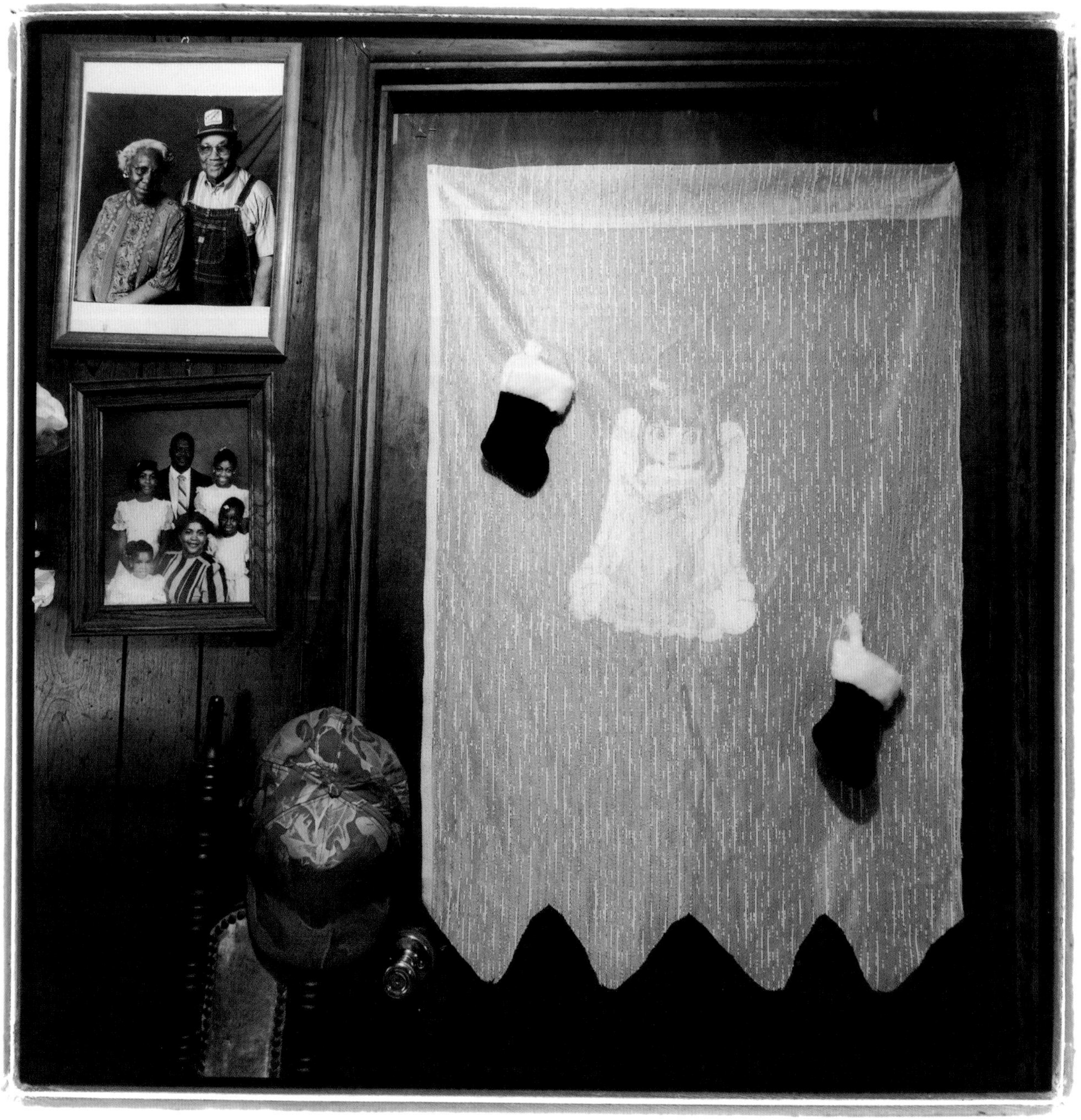

Angels

Christmas Tree

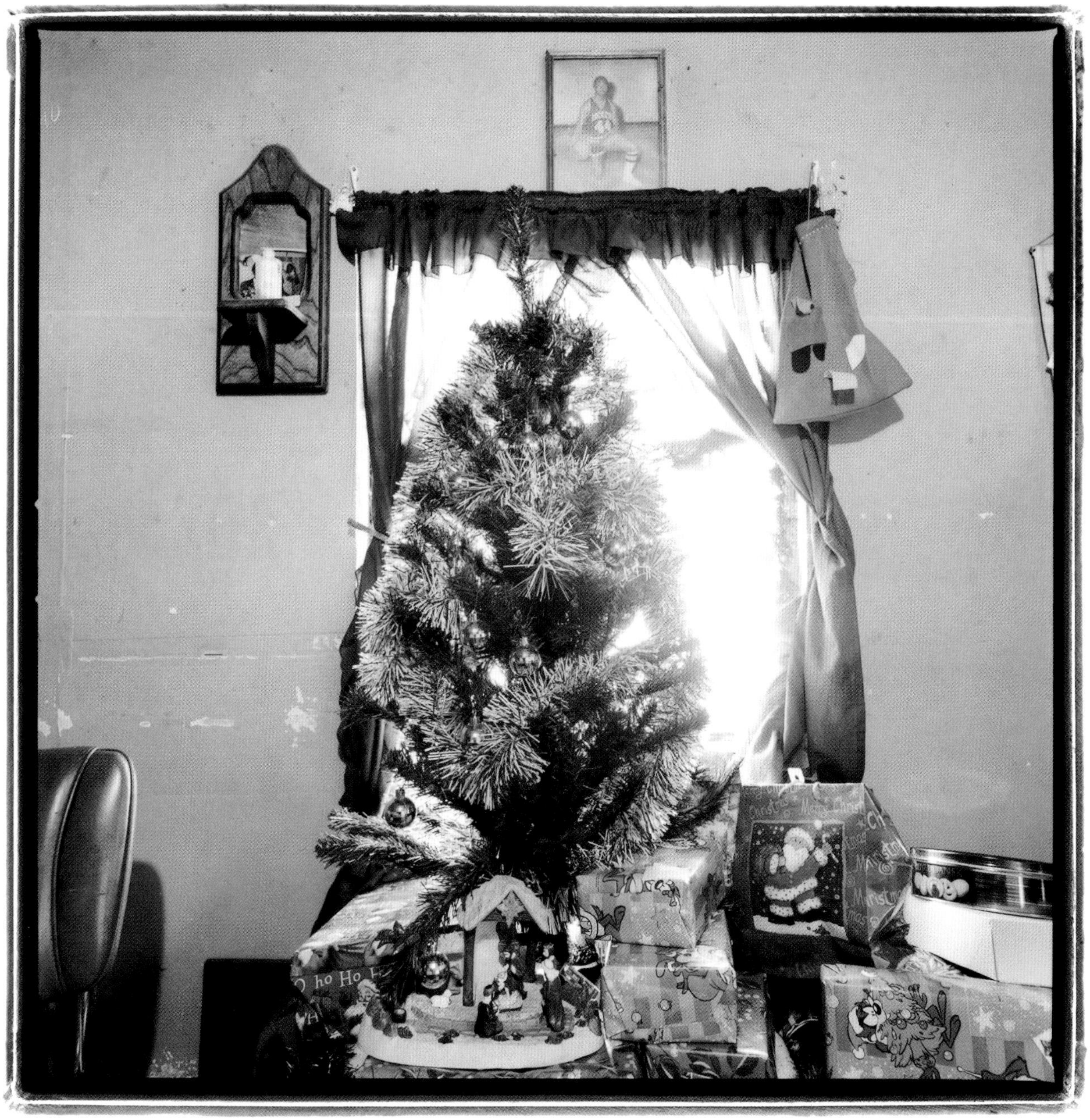

Big Hair

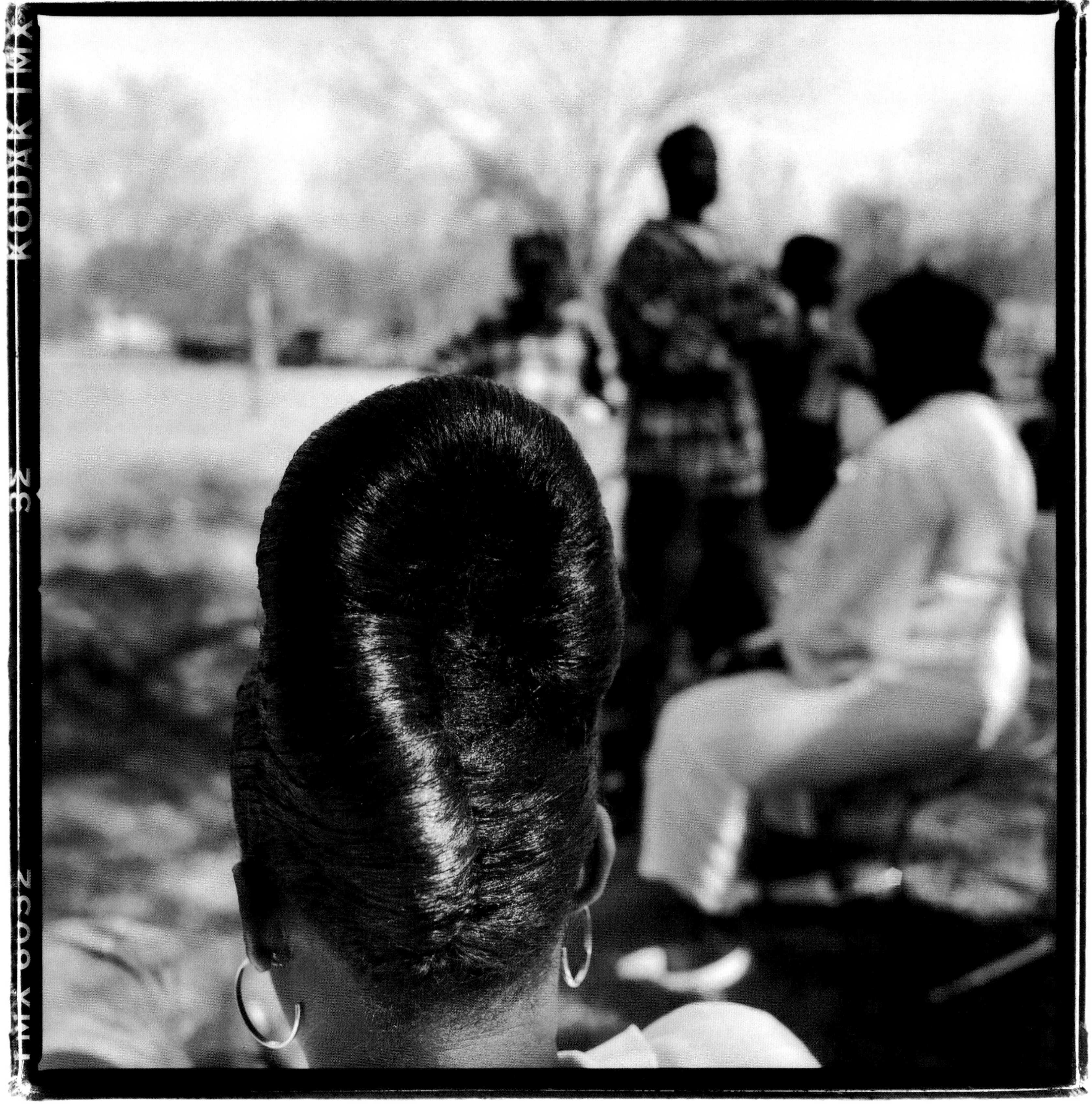

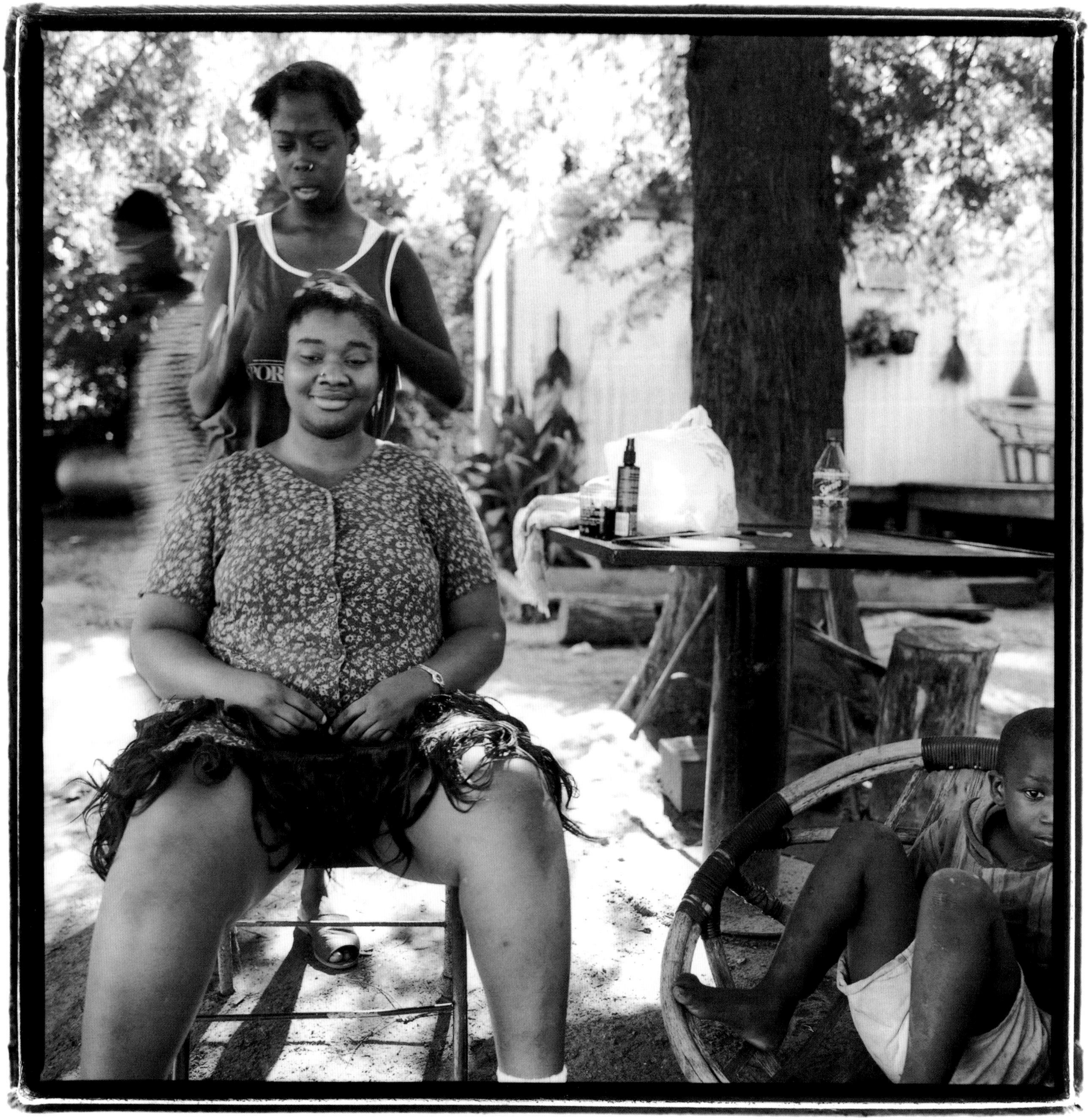

Extensions

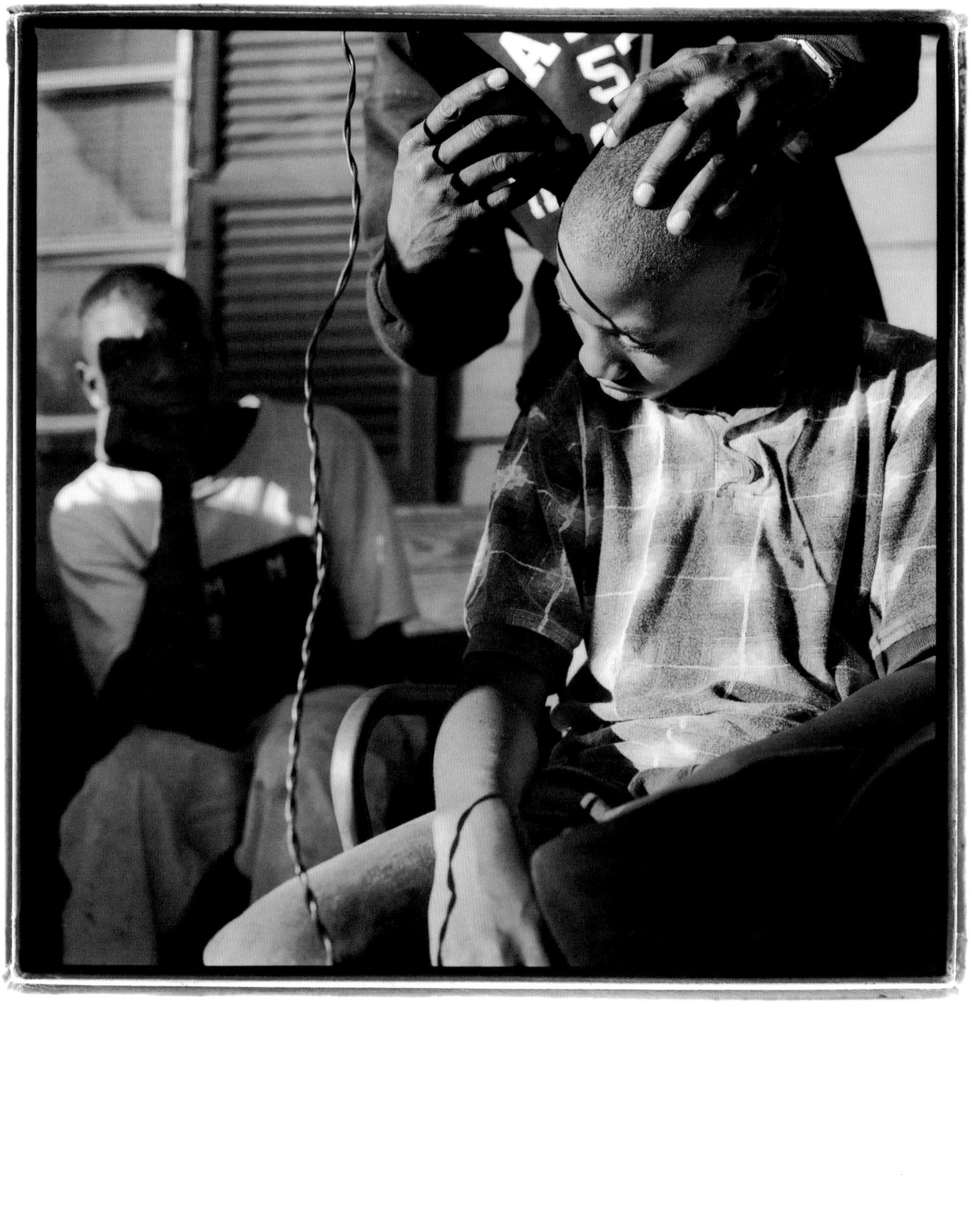

Haircut

Barber

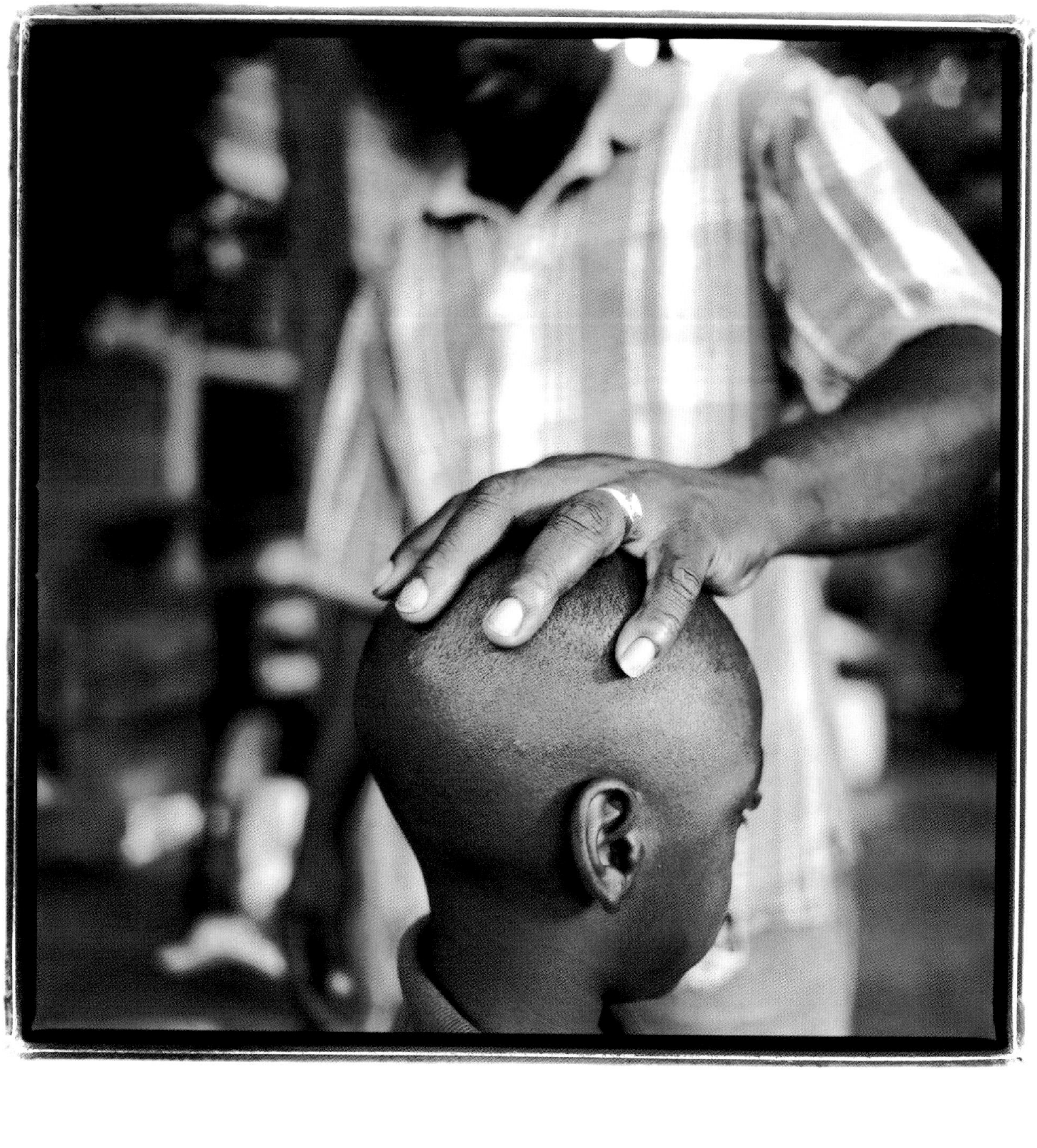

Church Porch

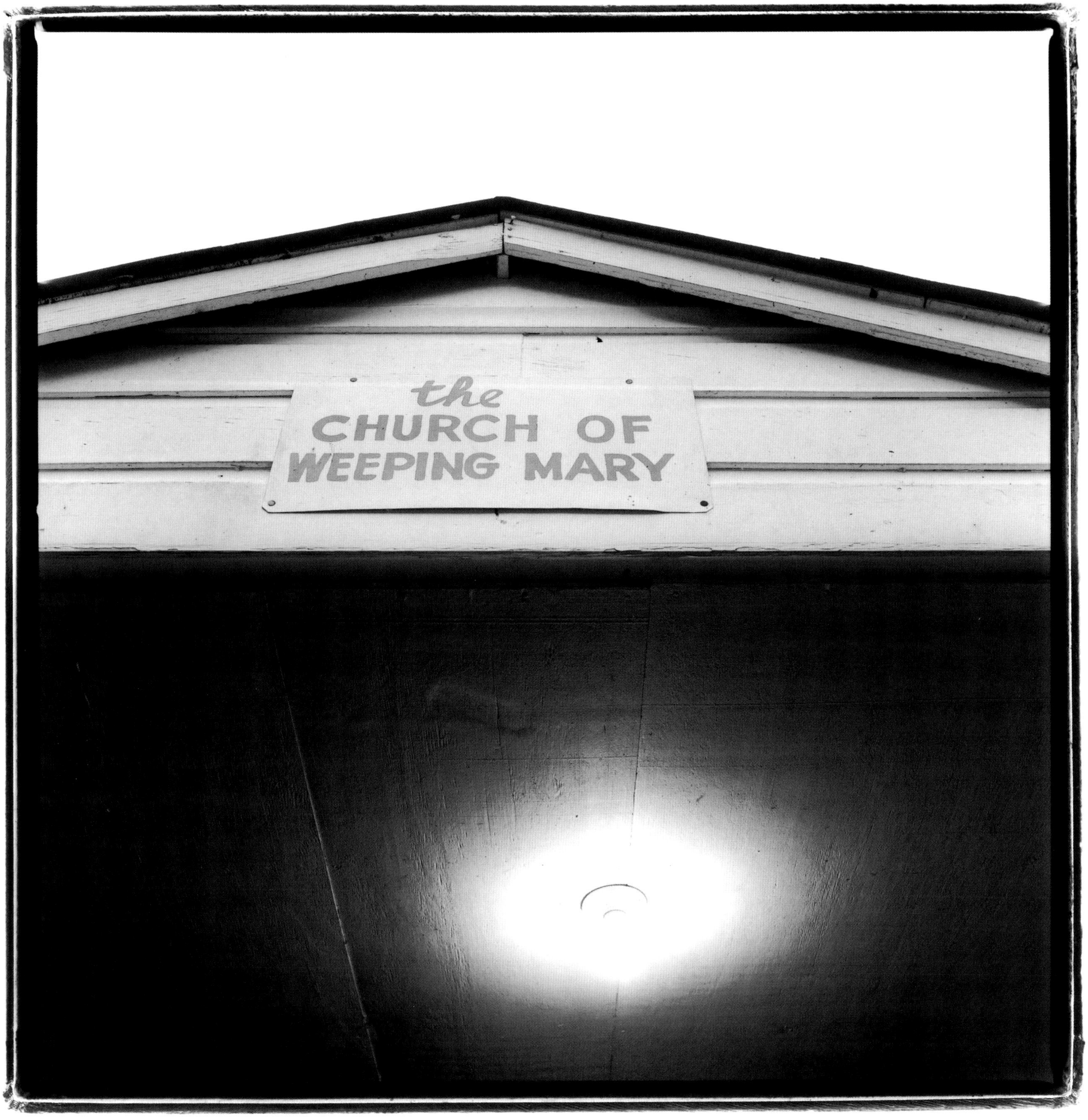
the
CHURCH OF
WEEPING MARY

Sisters

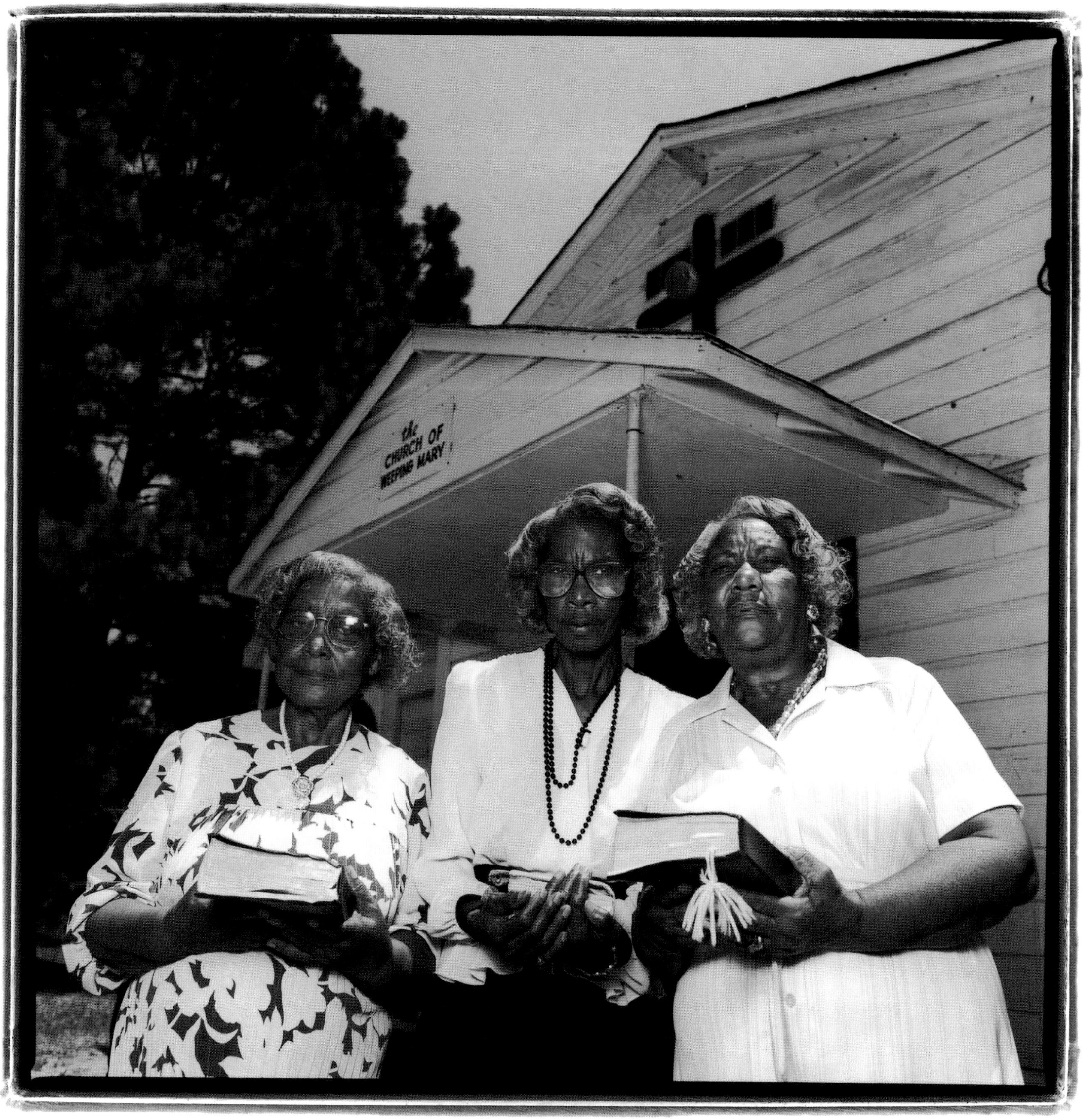
the
CHURCH OF
WEEPING MARY

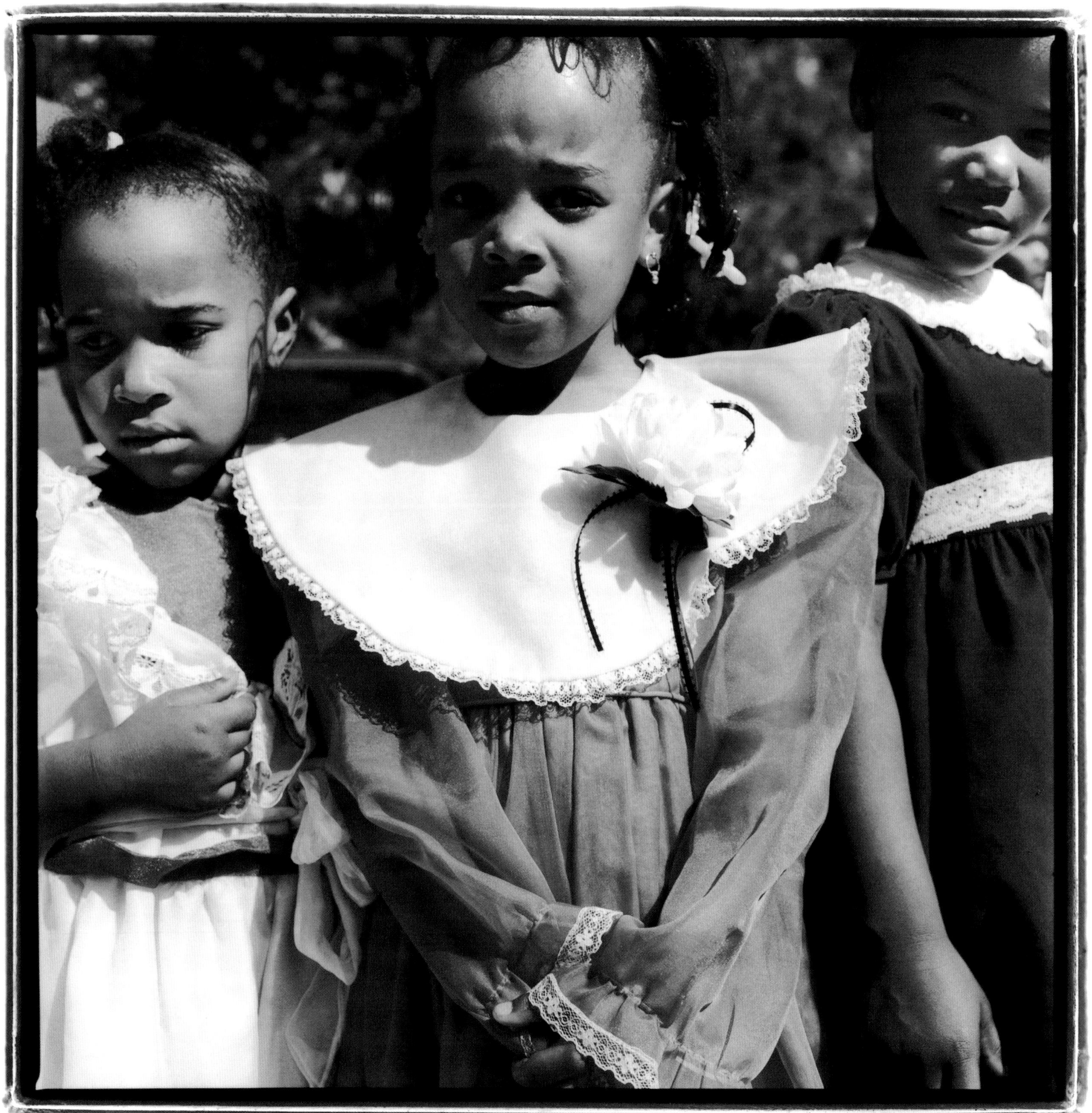

Sunday Dresses

Demitria's Shoes

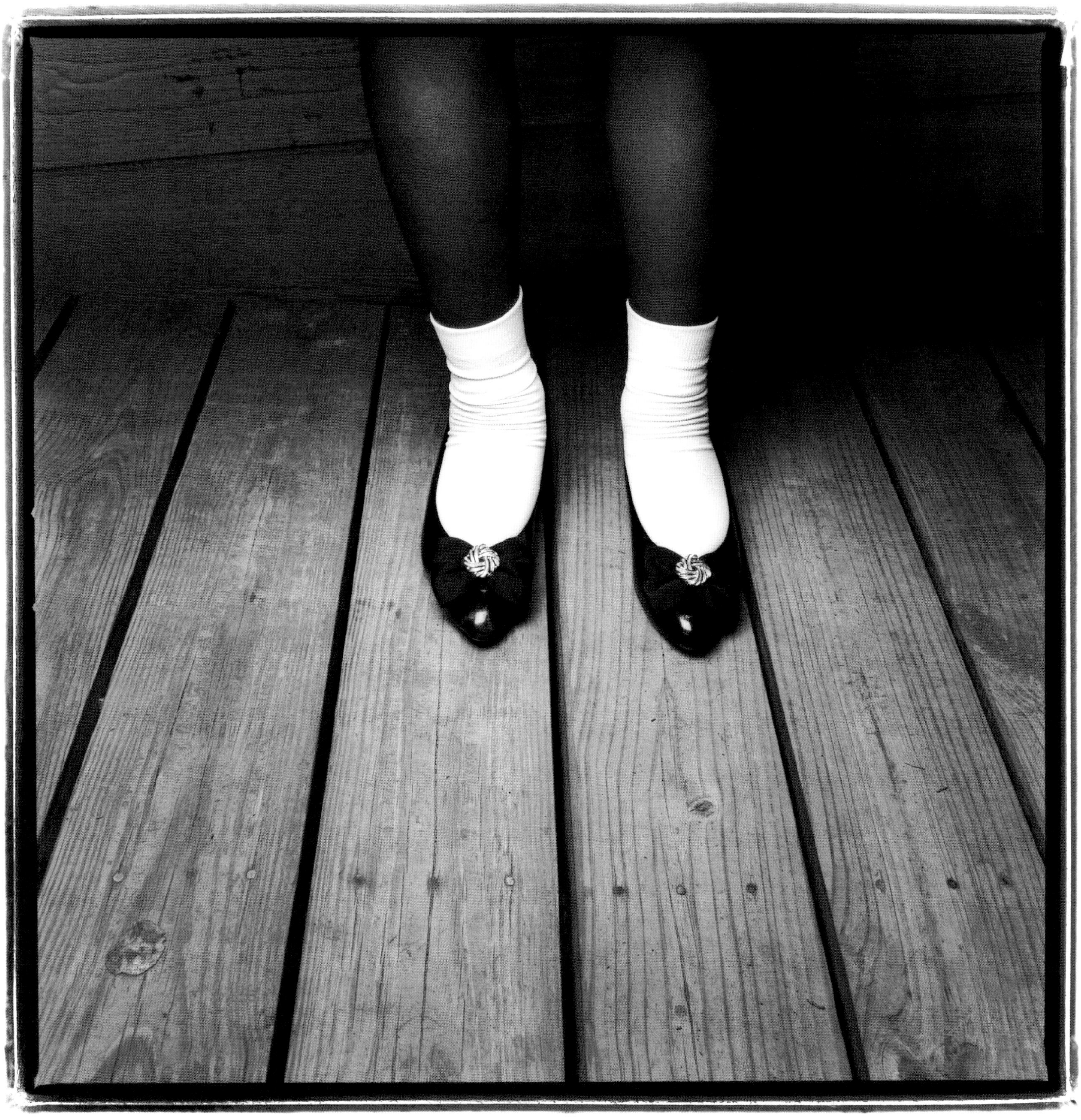

Sunday Shadow

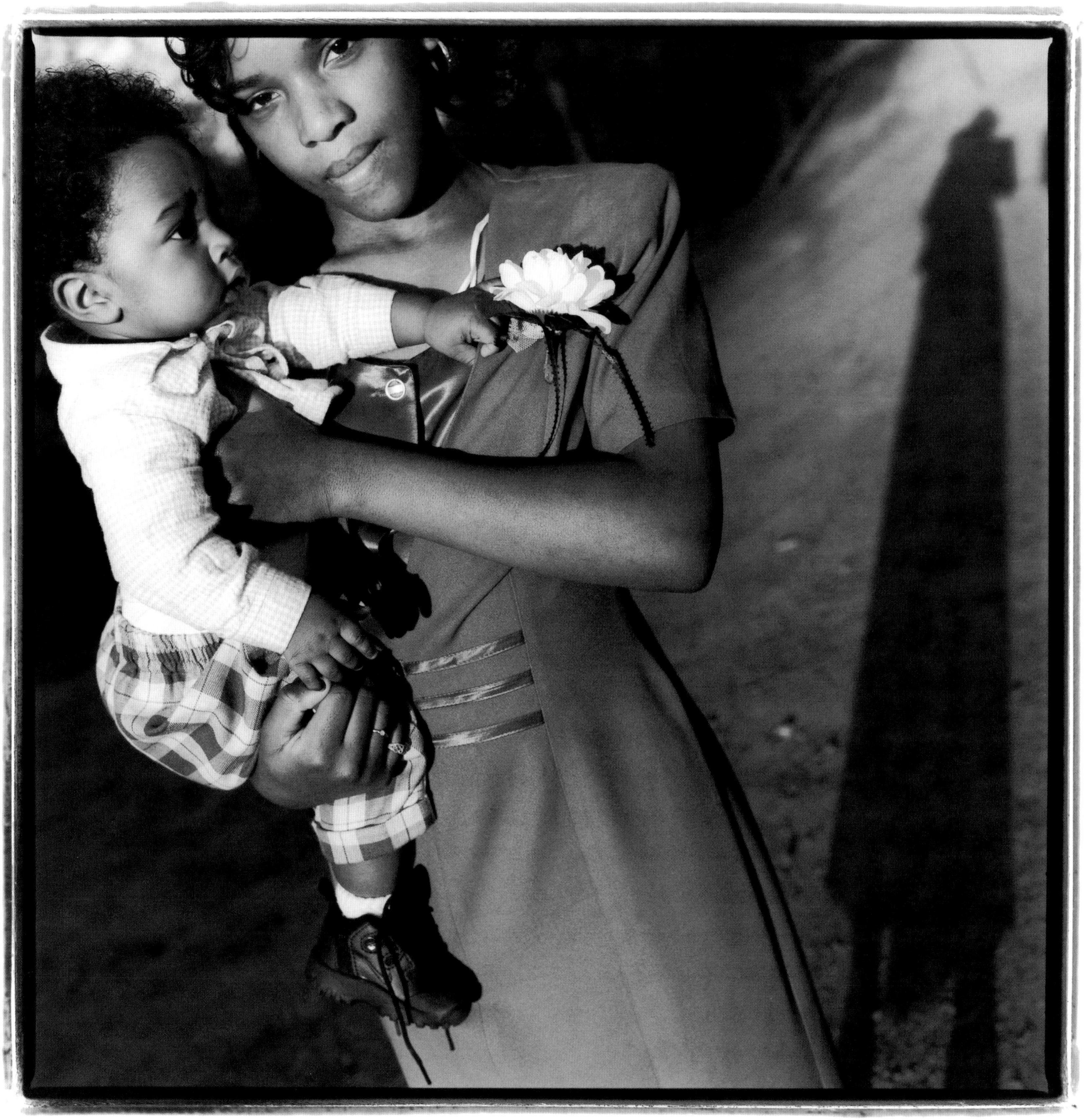

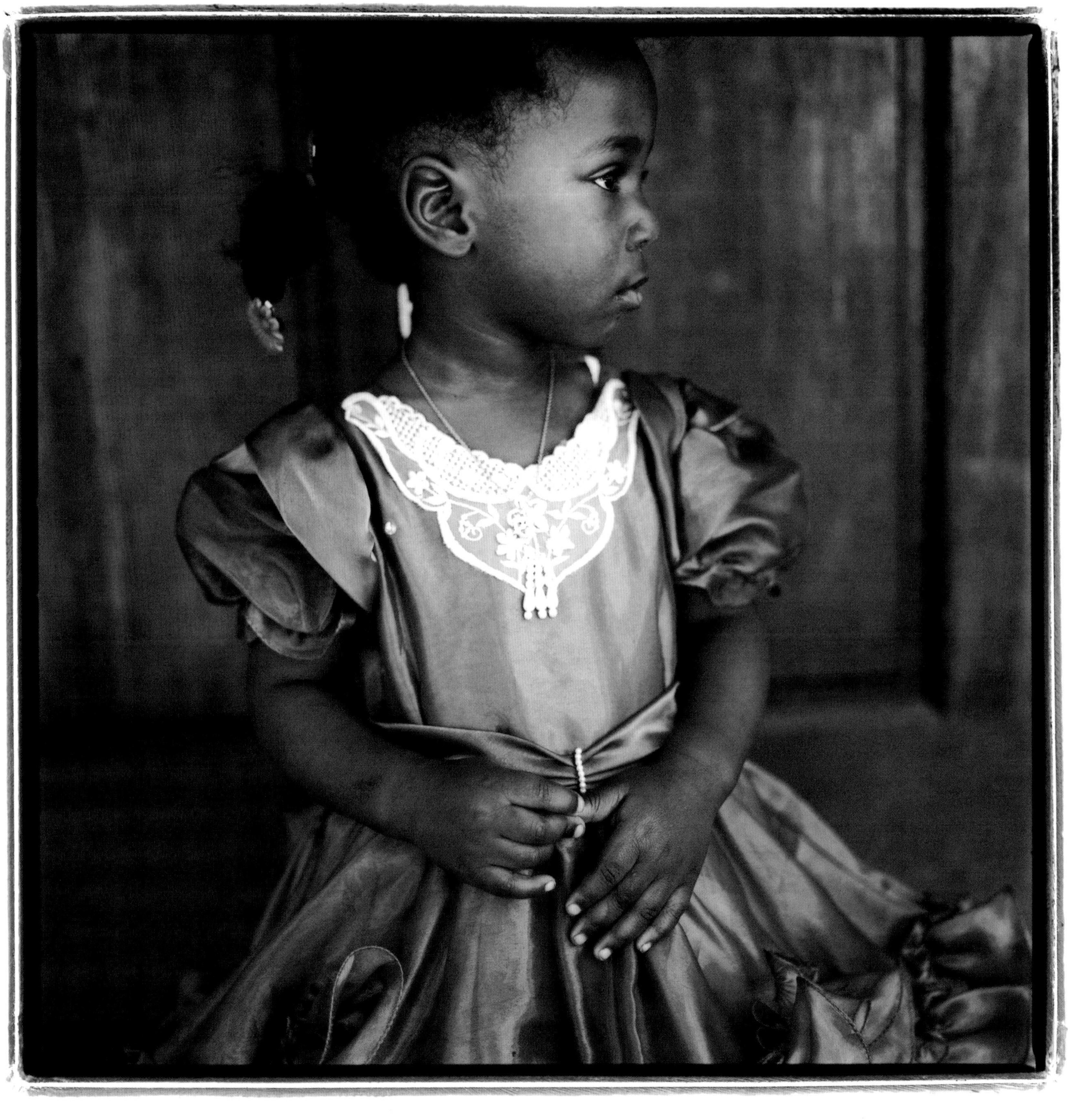

Polly

Easter Sunday

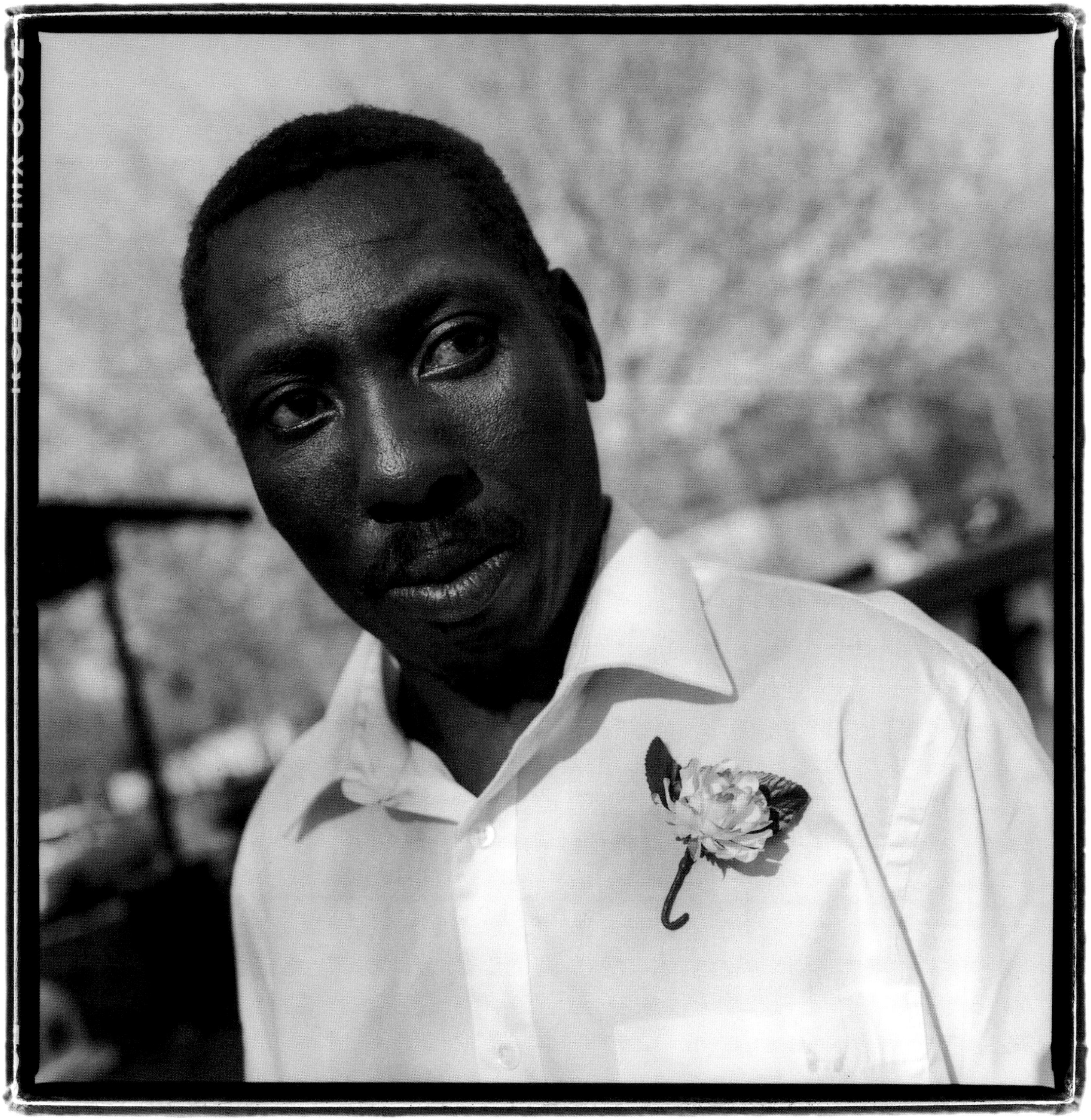

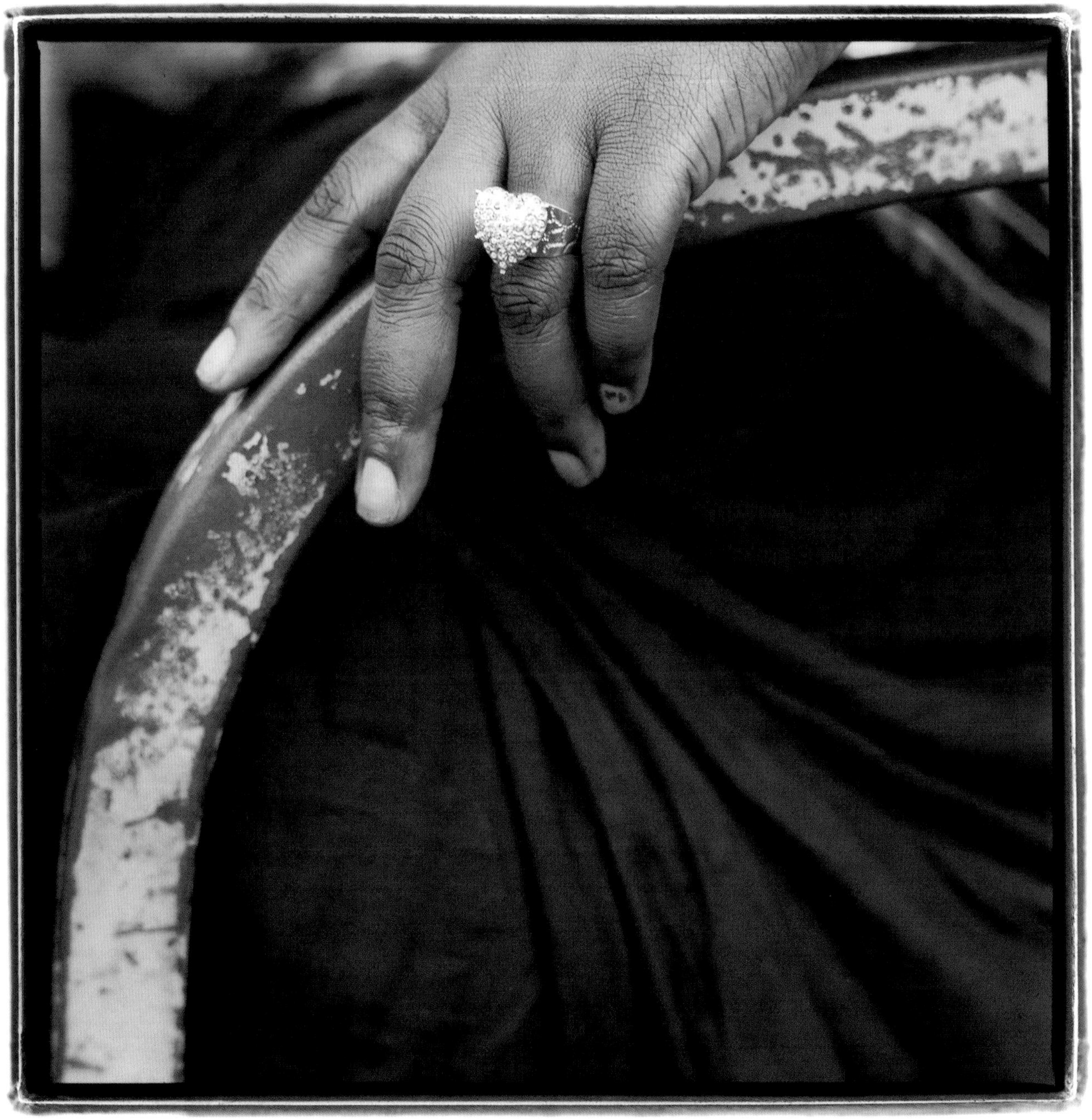

Heart Ring

Earring

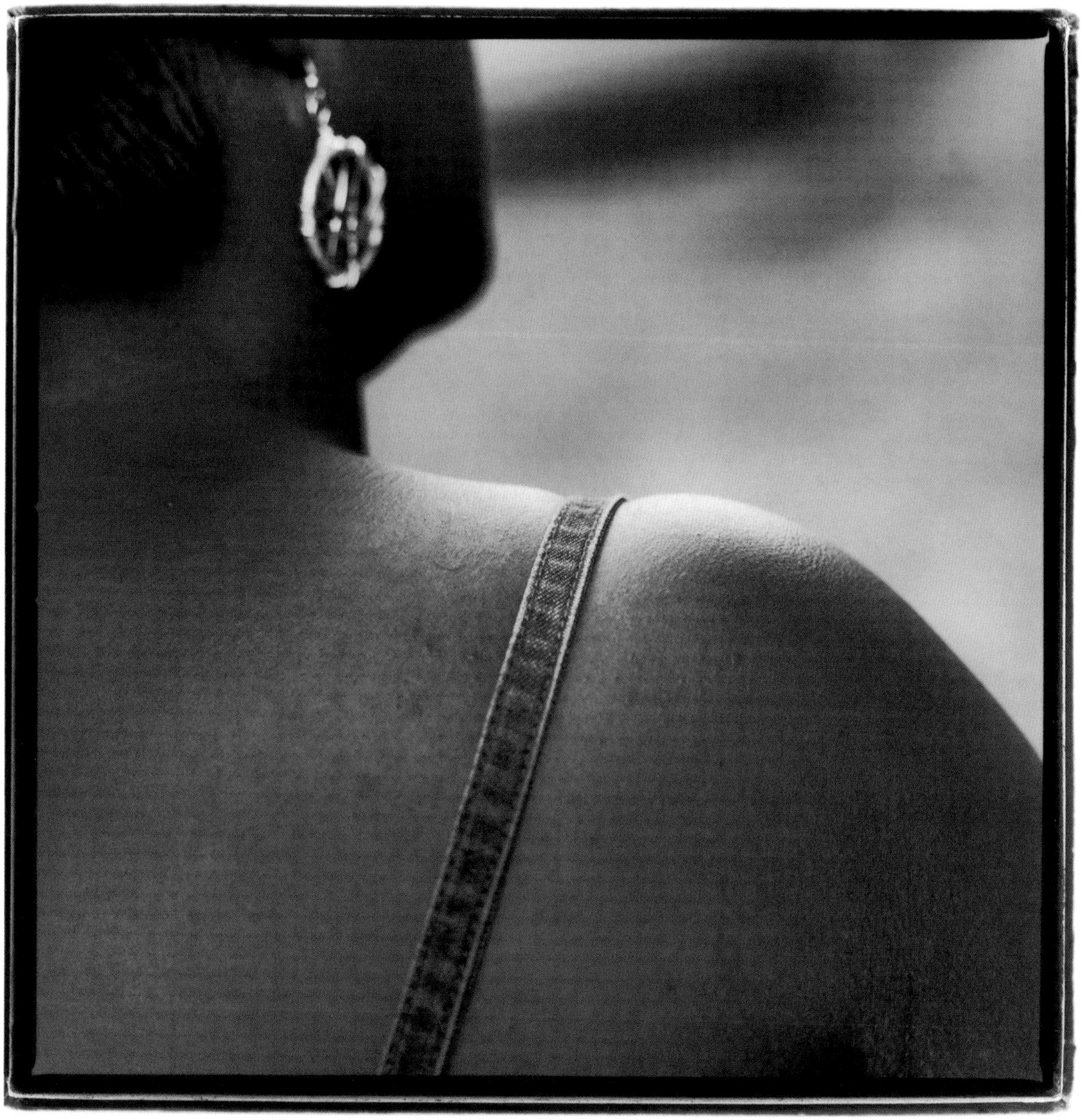

Bible School

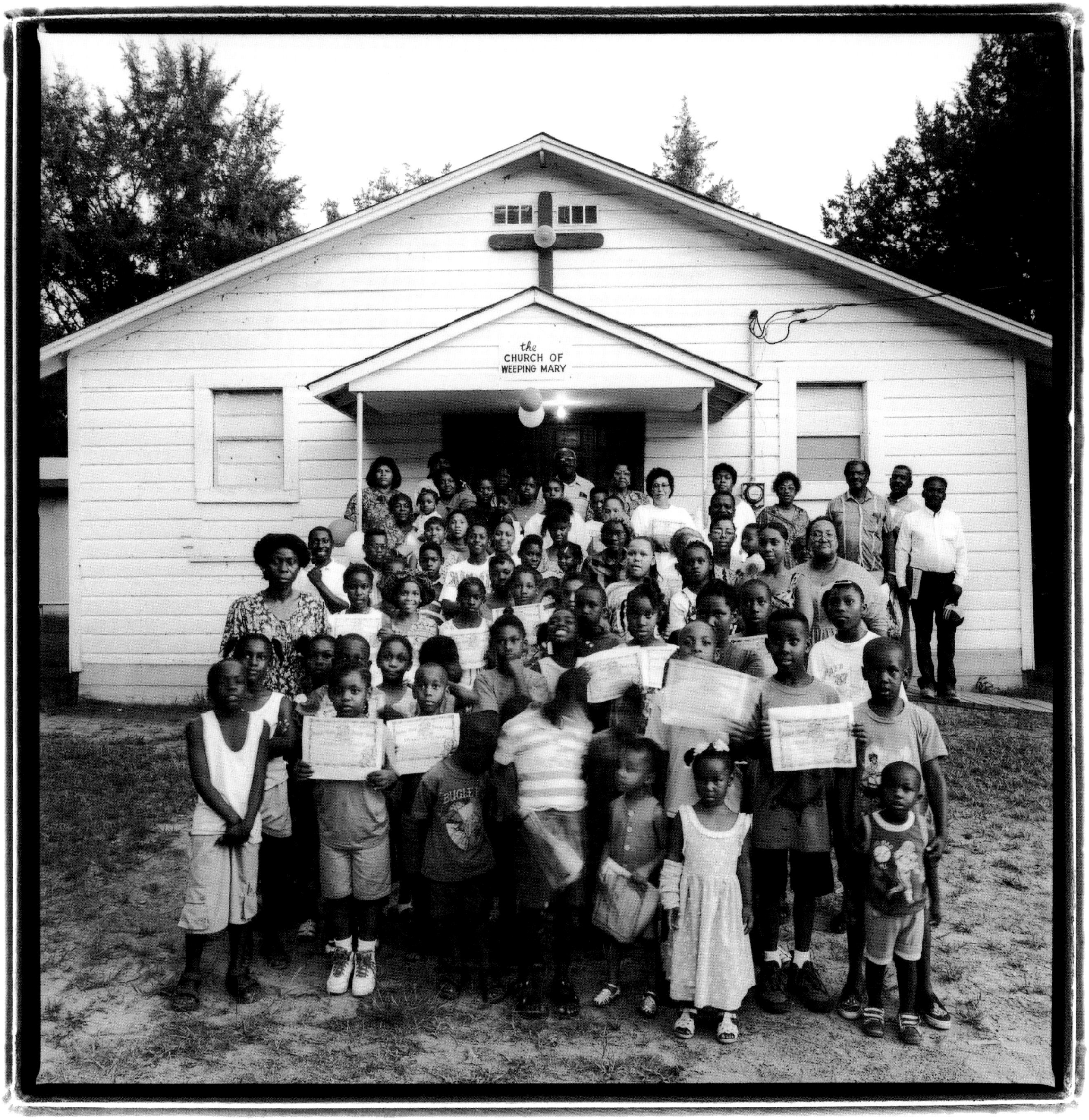
the
CHURCH OF
WEEPING MARY

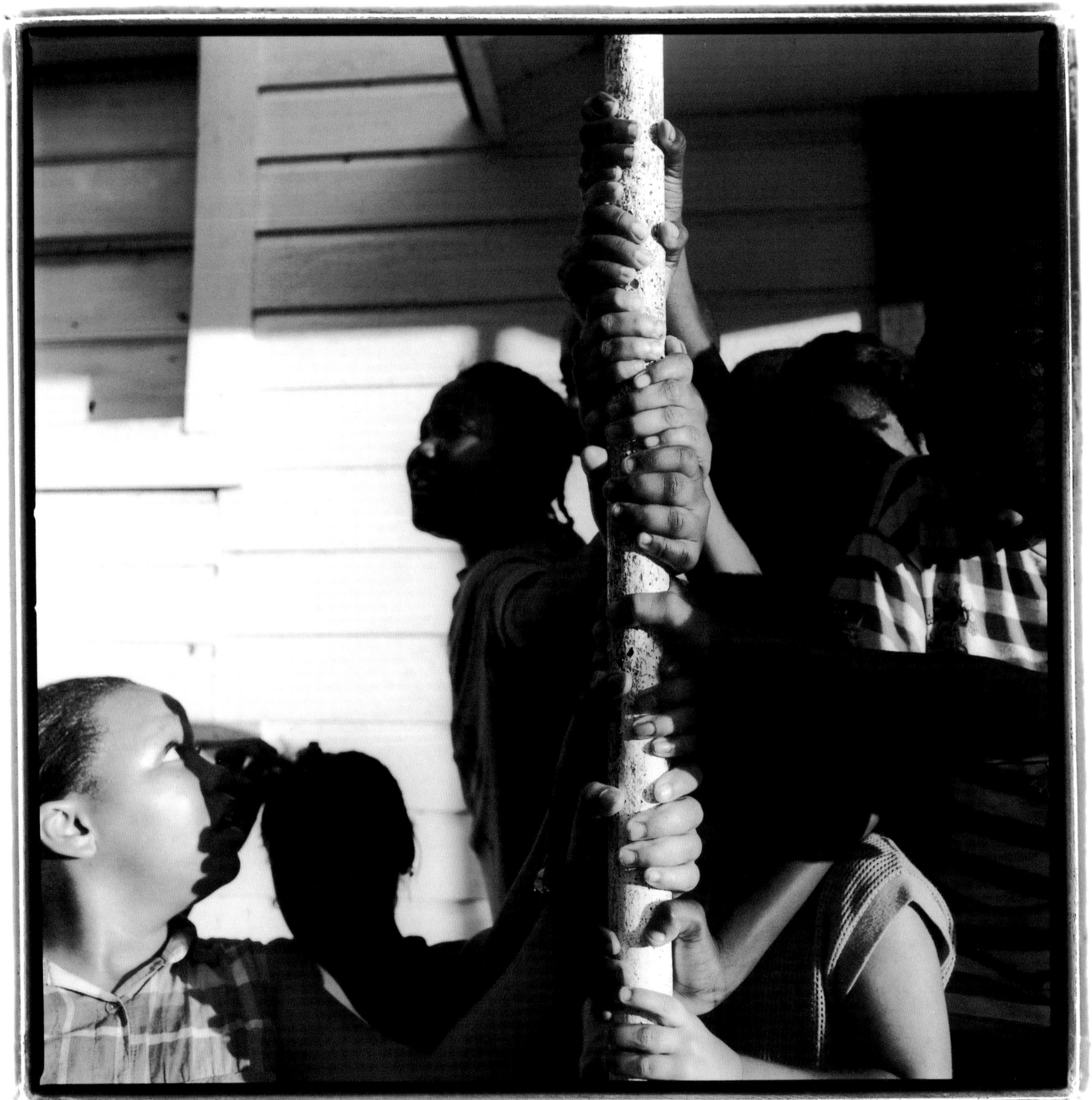

Hands

Church Hat

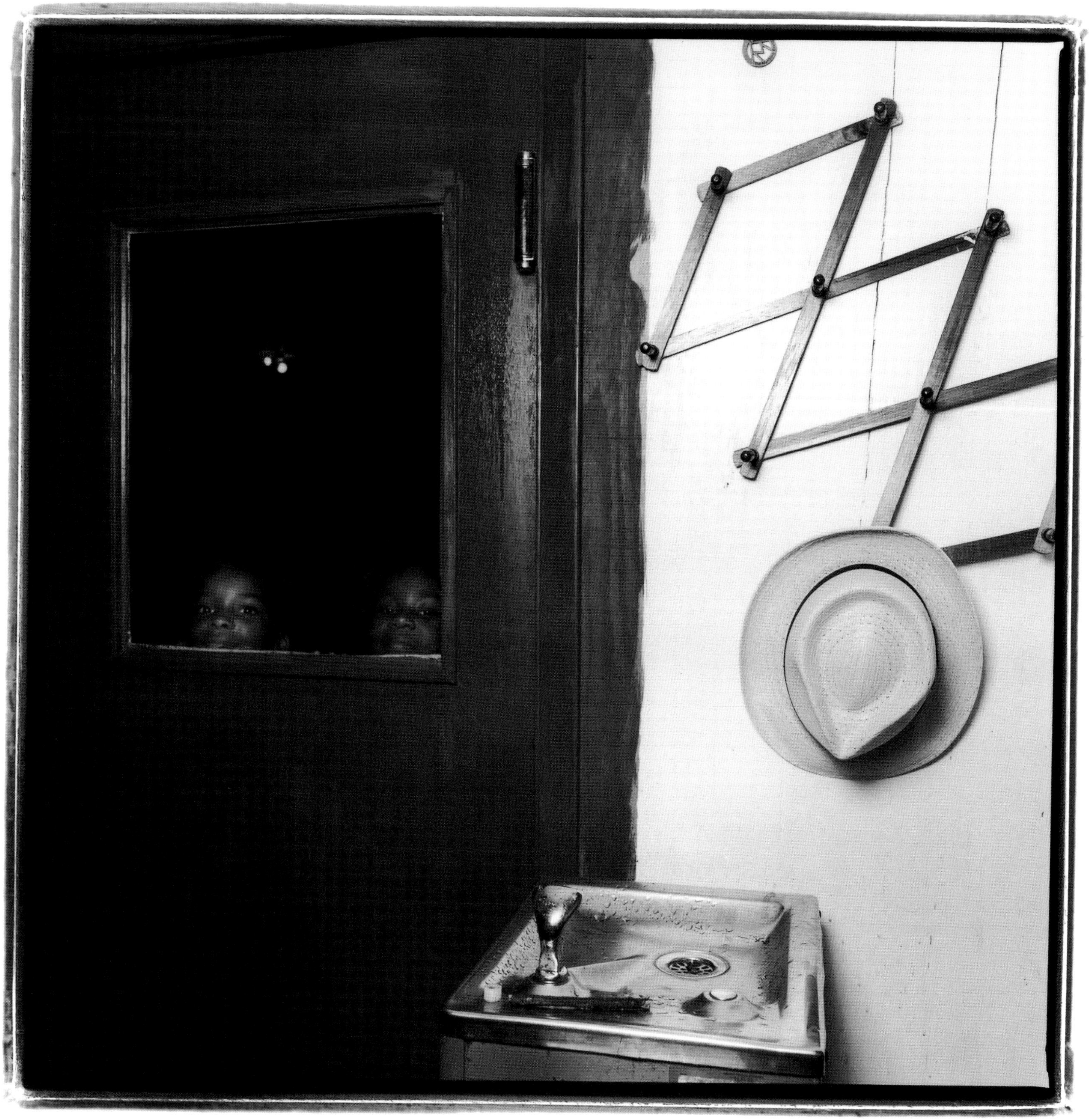

118

Martin Luther King Jr. Fan

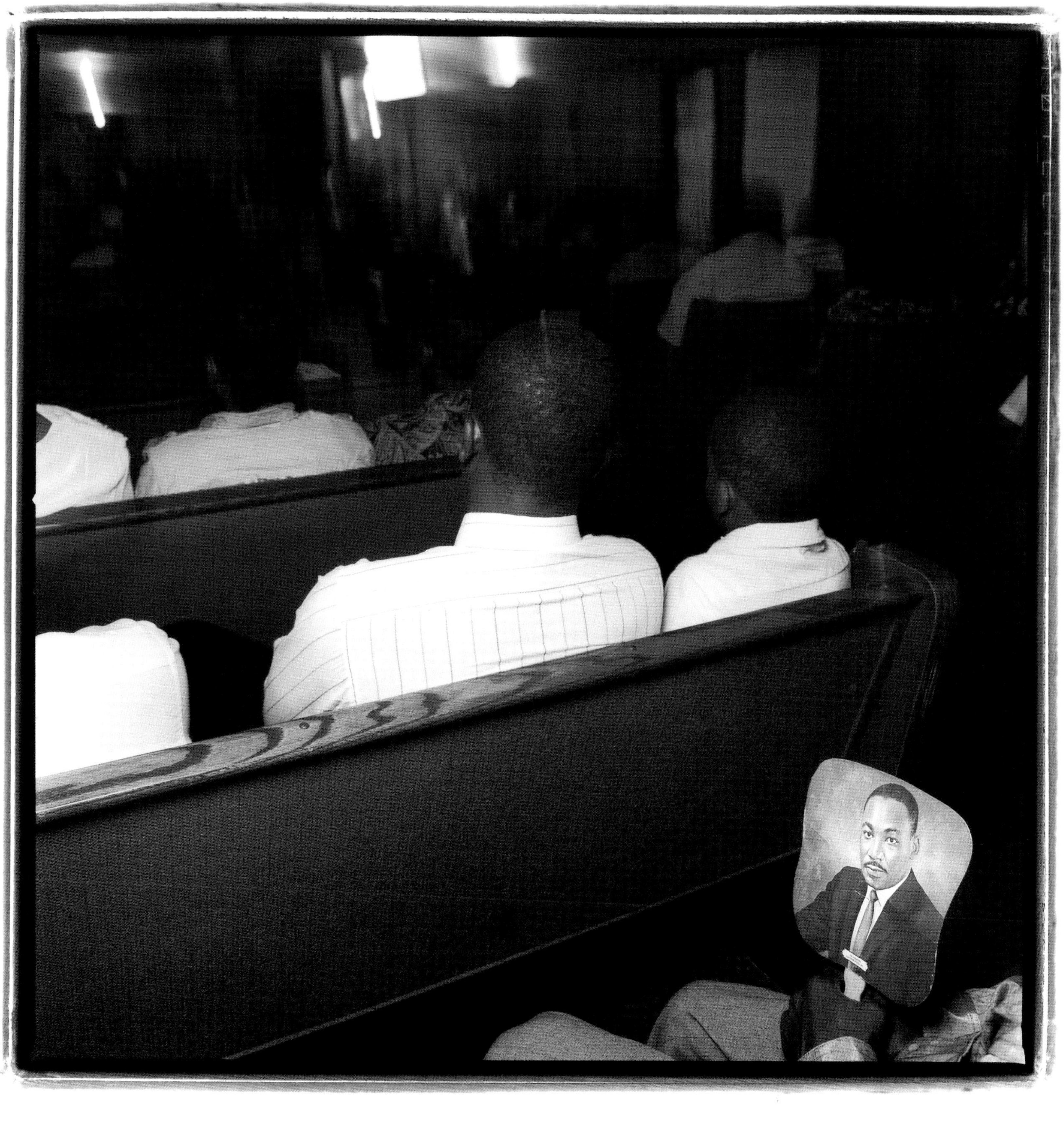

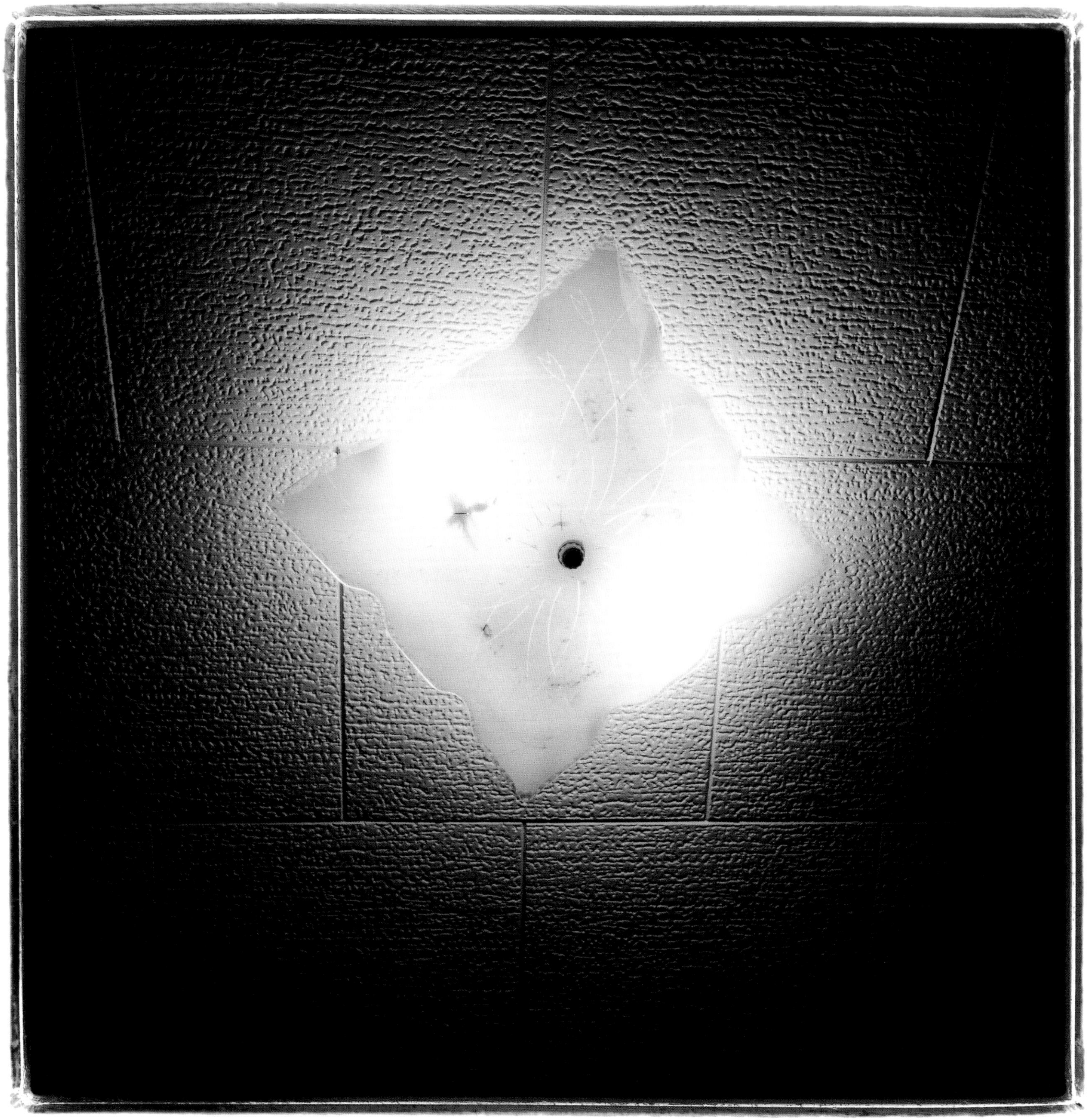

Wasp

122

Church Service

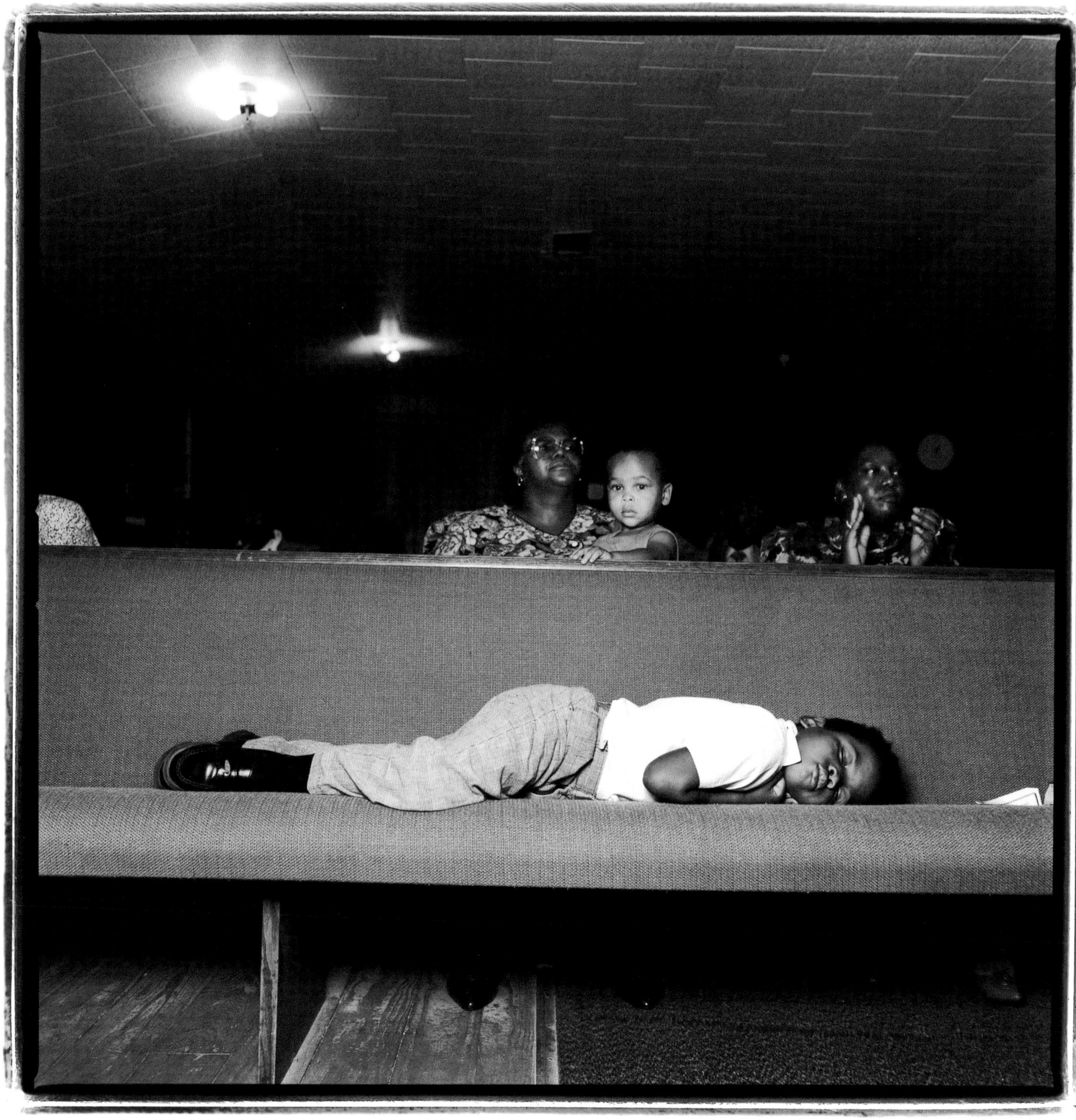

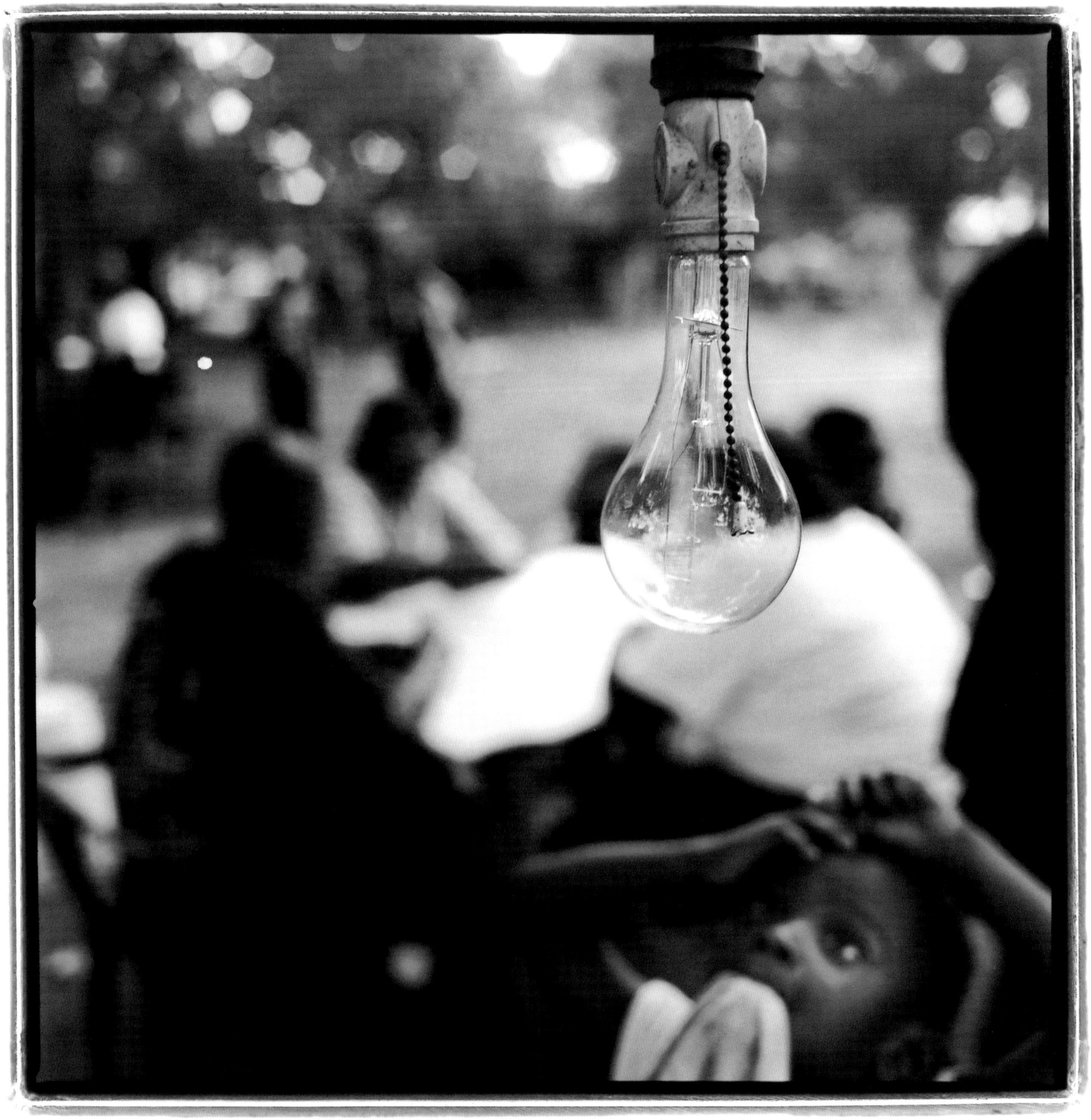

Light Bulb

Flower Suit

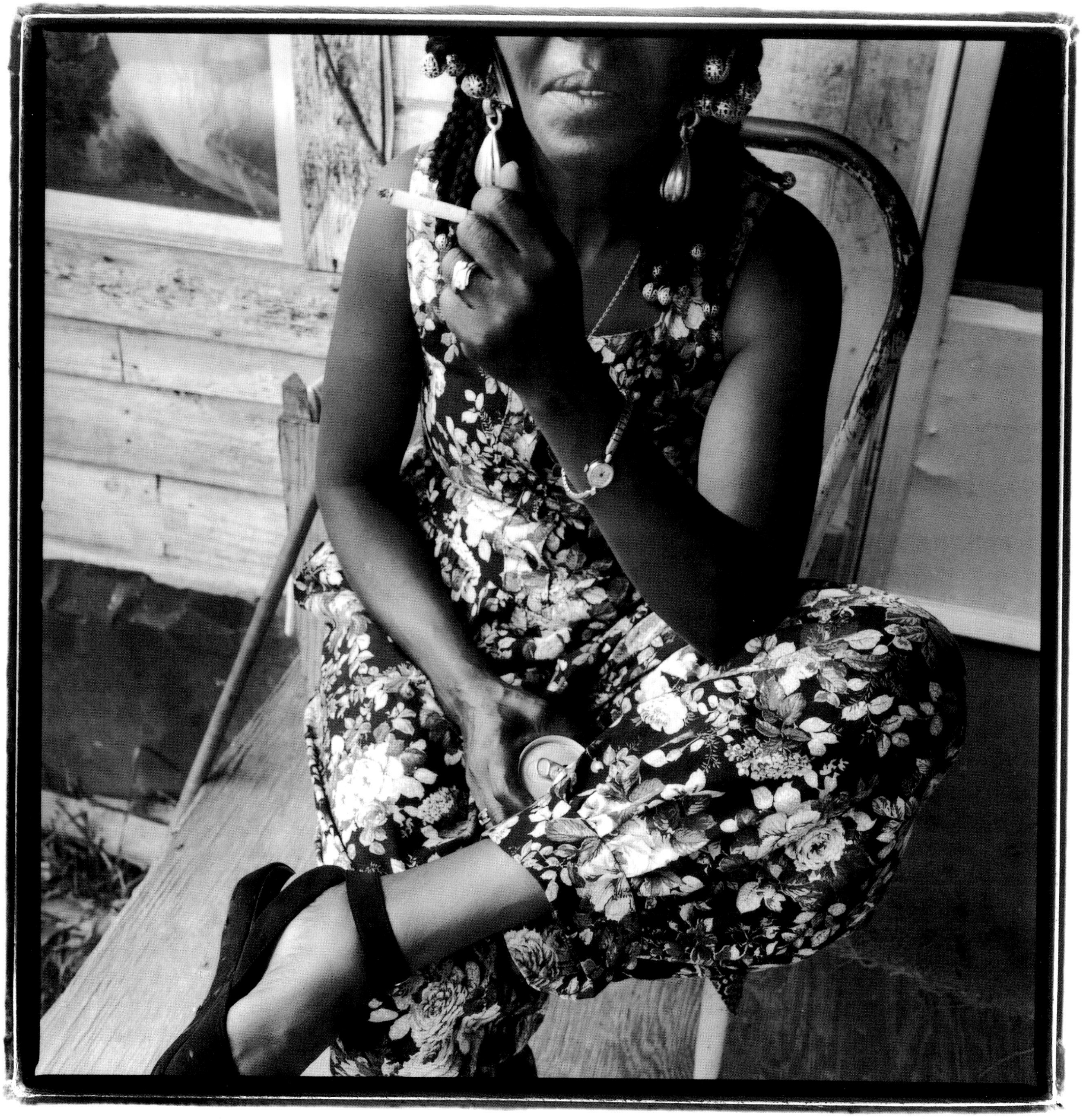

Mama's Dress

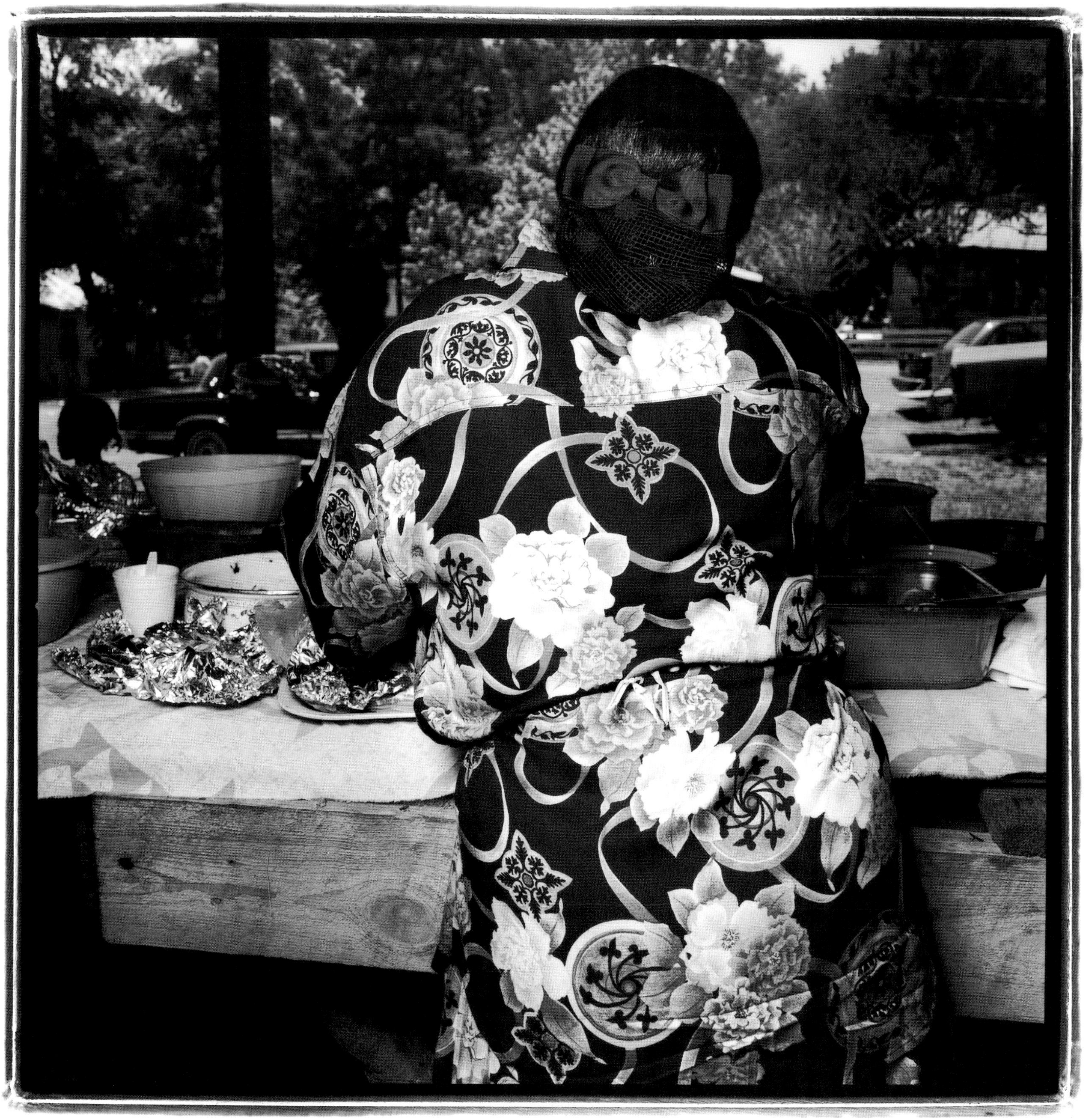

Loretta's Diary

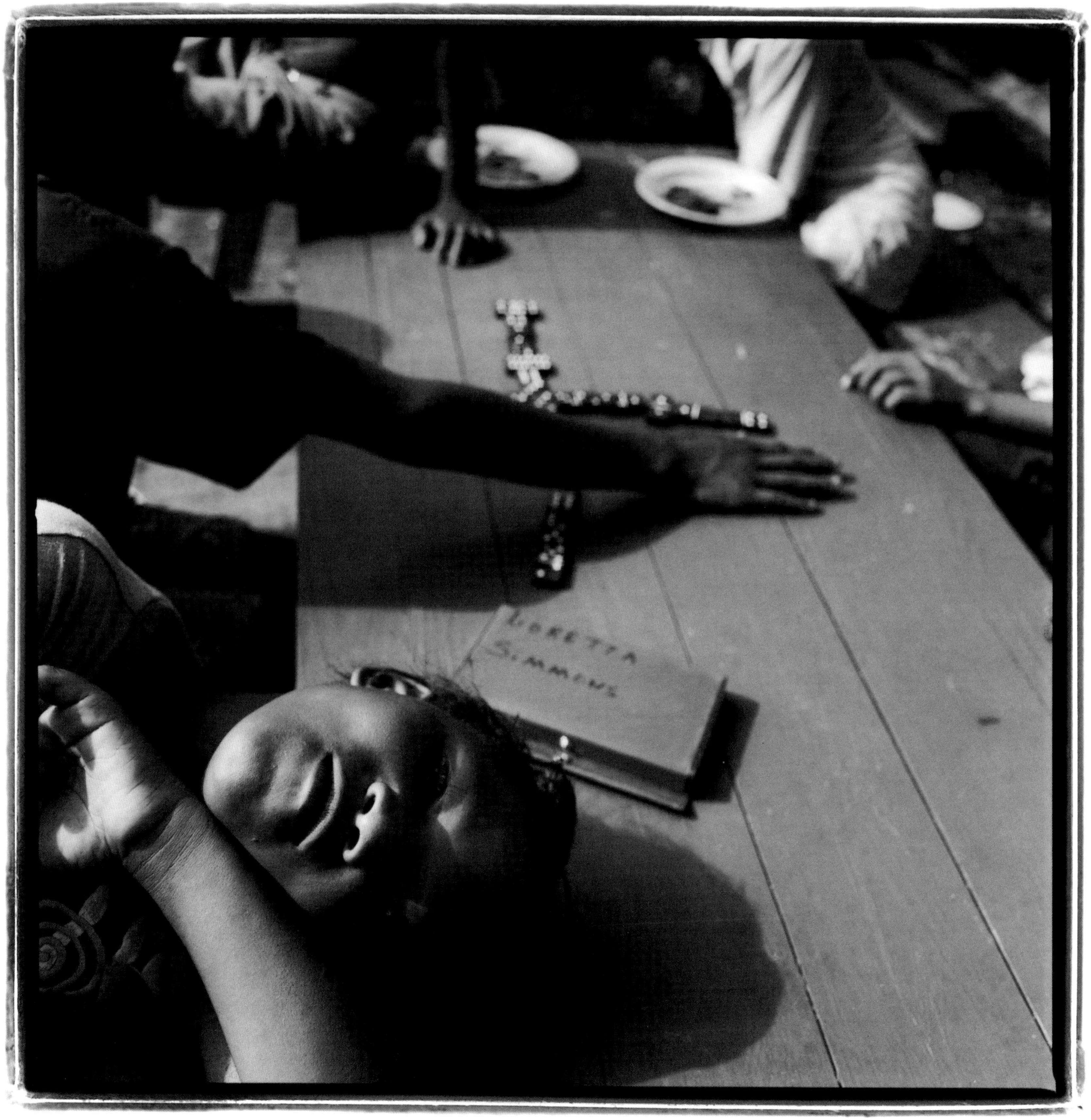
LORETTA
SIMMONS

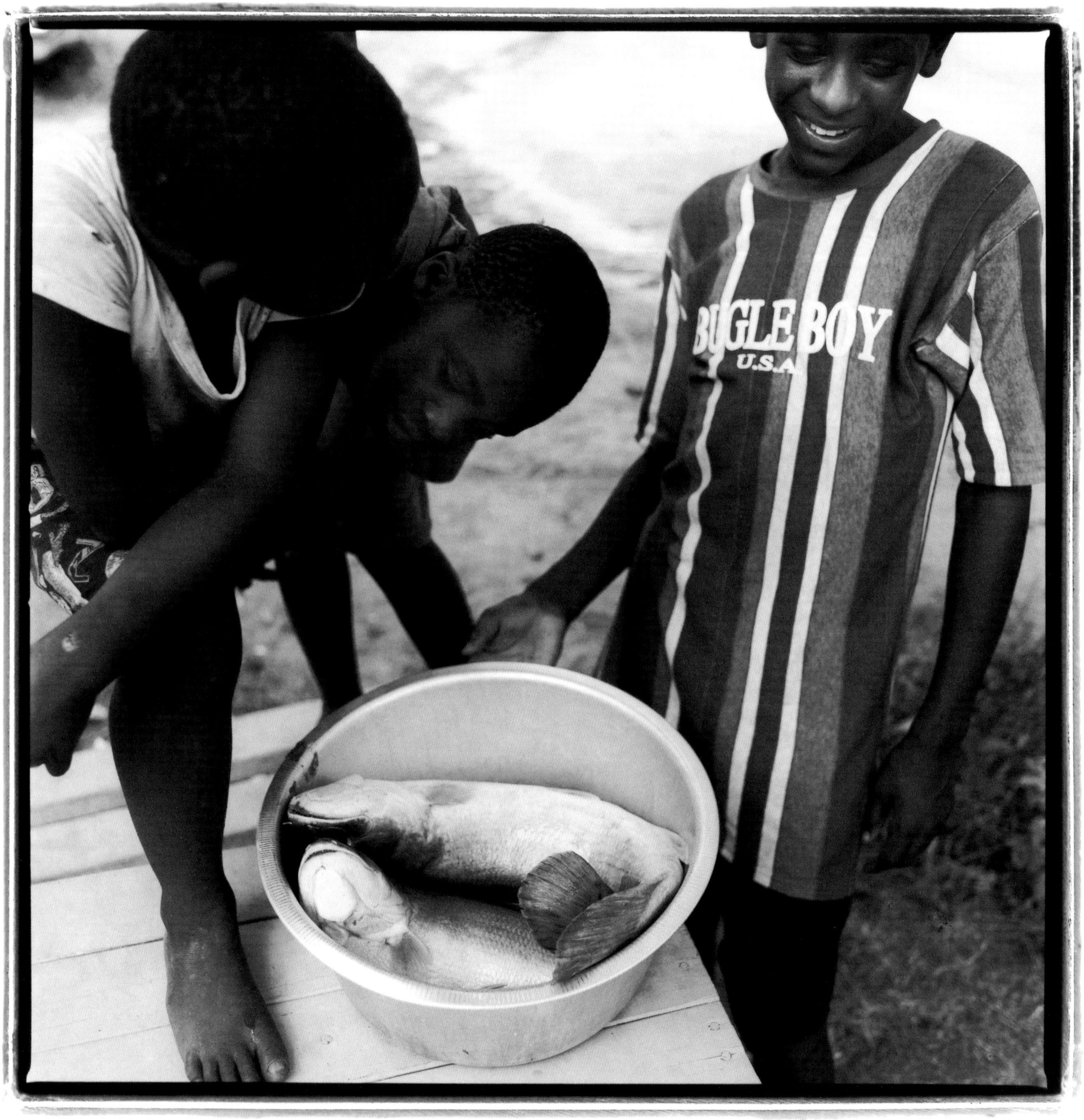
BUGLE BOY
U.S.A.

Bugle Boy

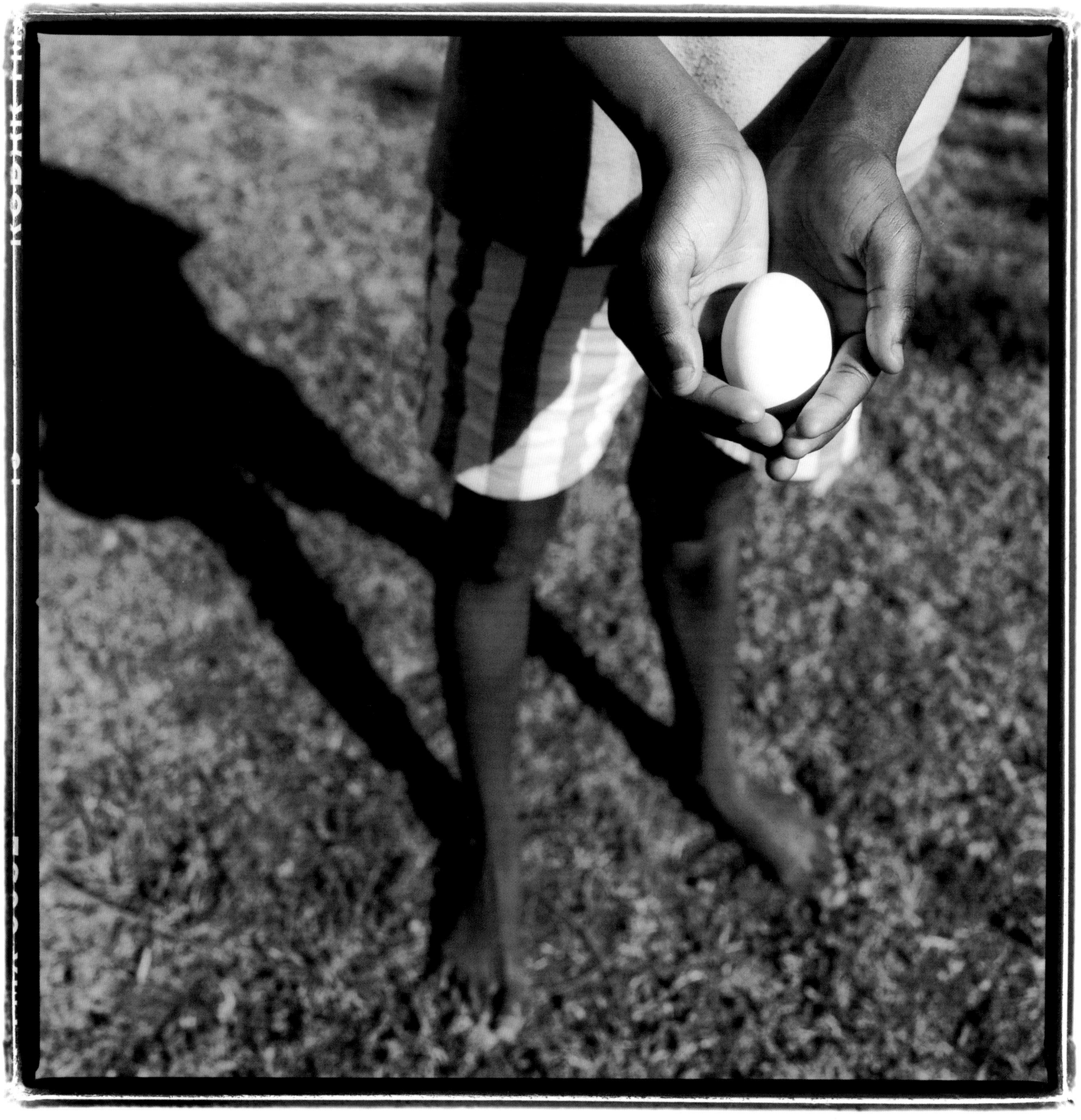

Easter Egg

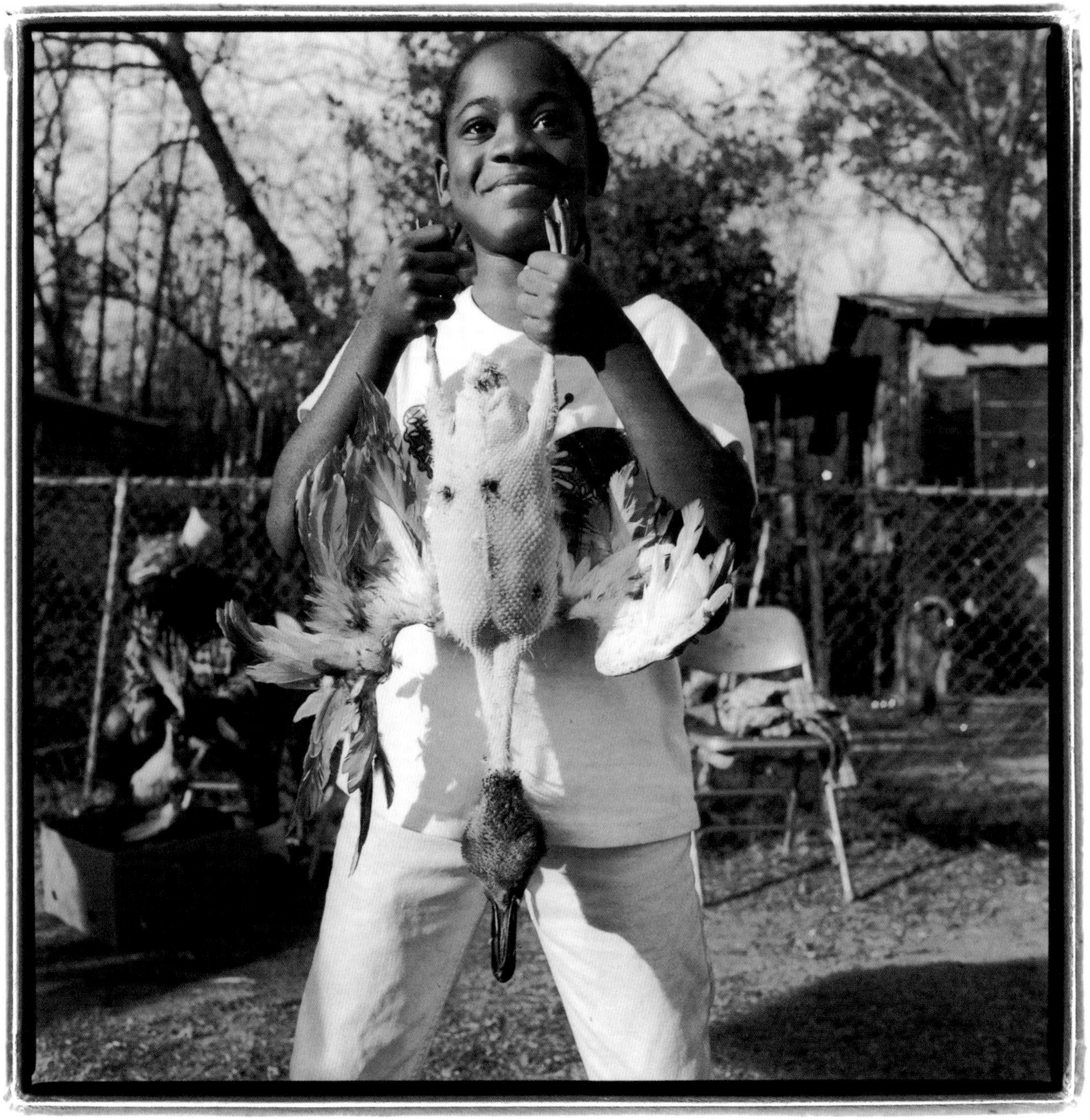

Duck

Duck Wing

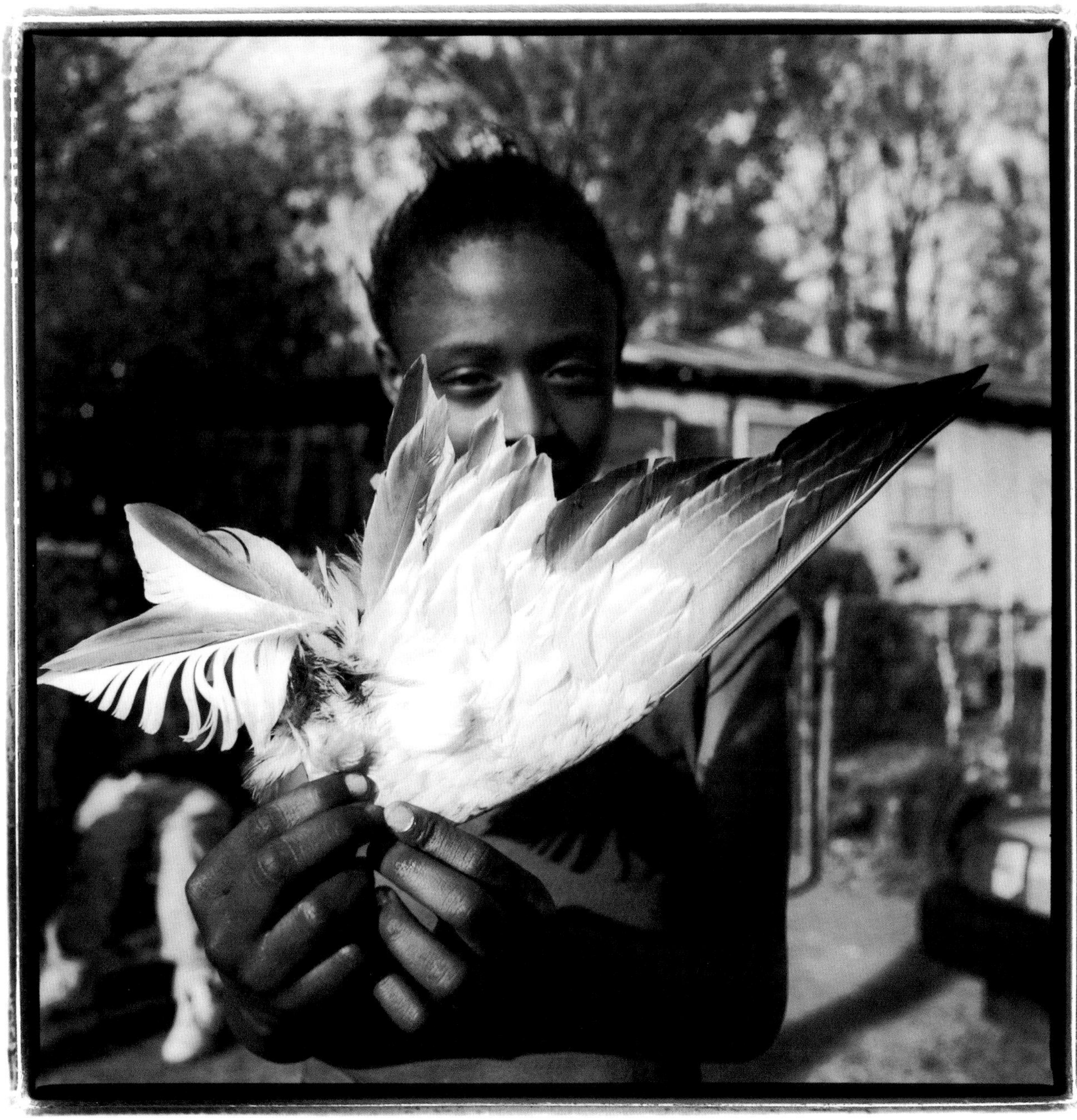

Duck Neck

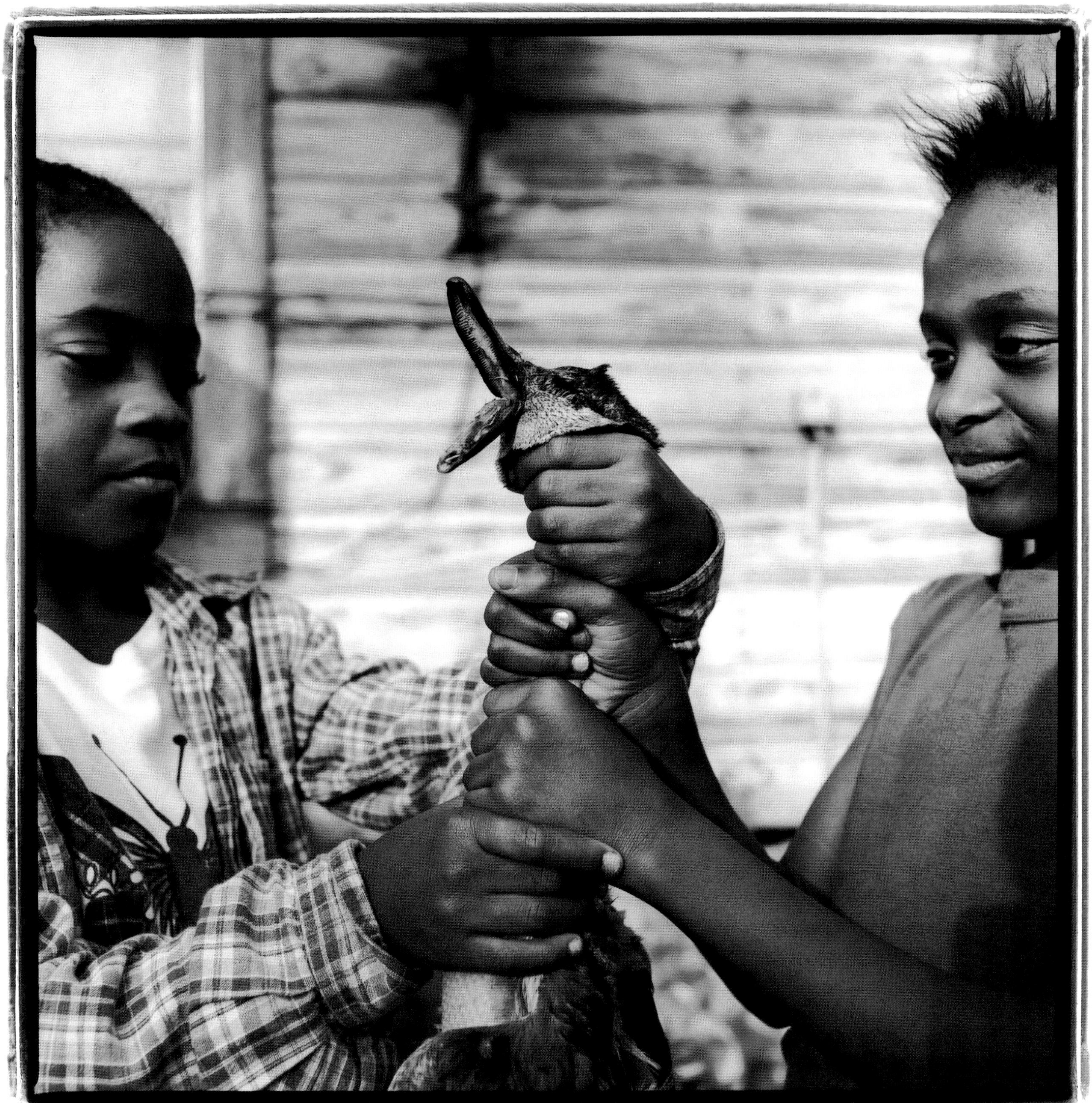

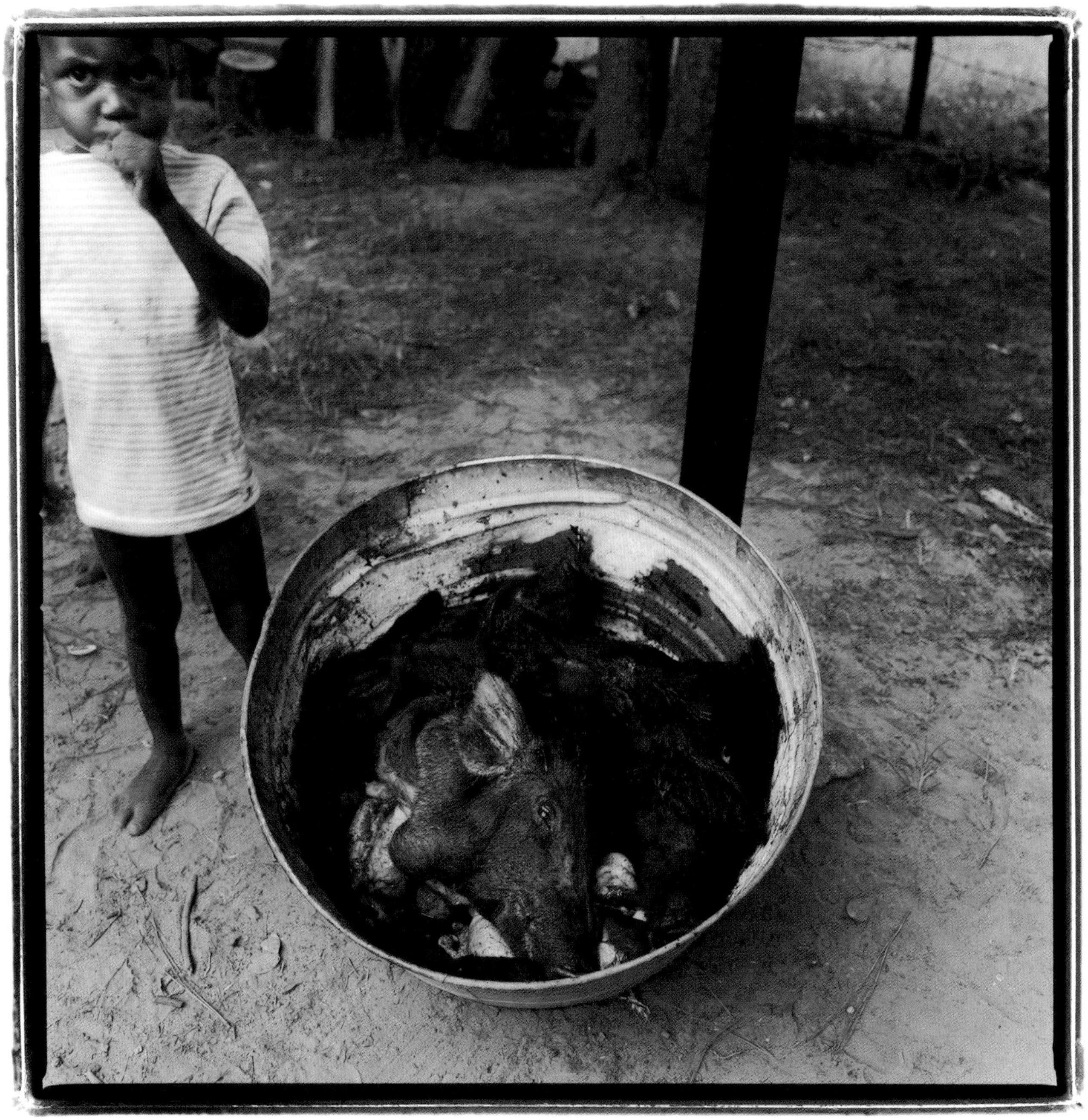

Wild Hog

Wild Hog

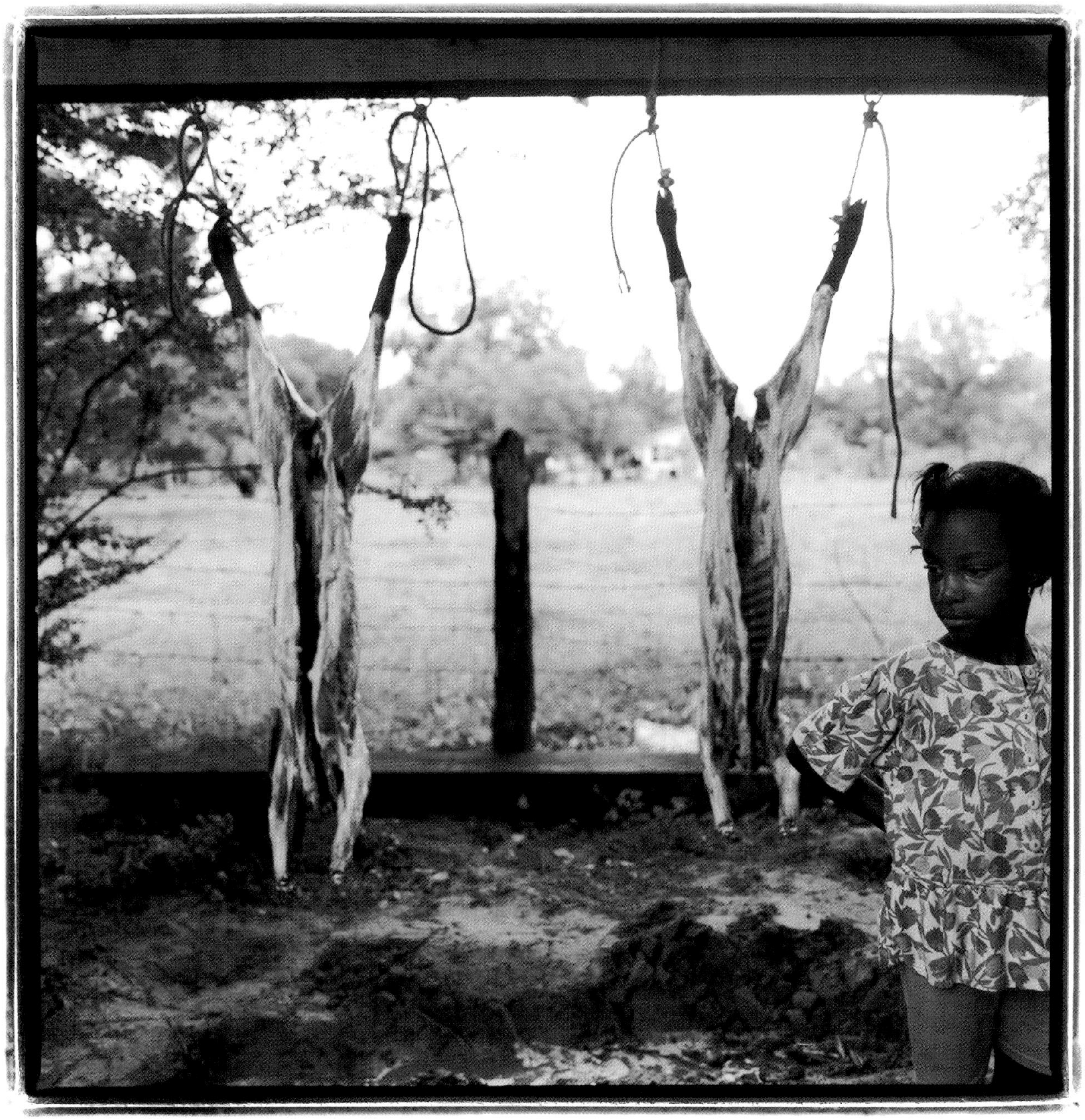

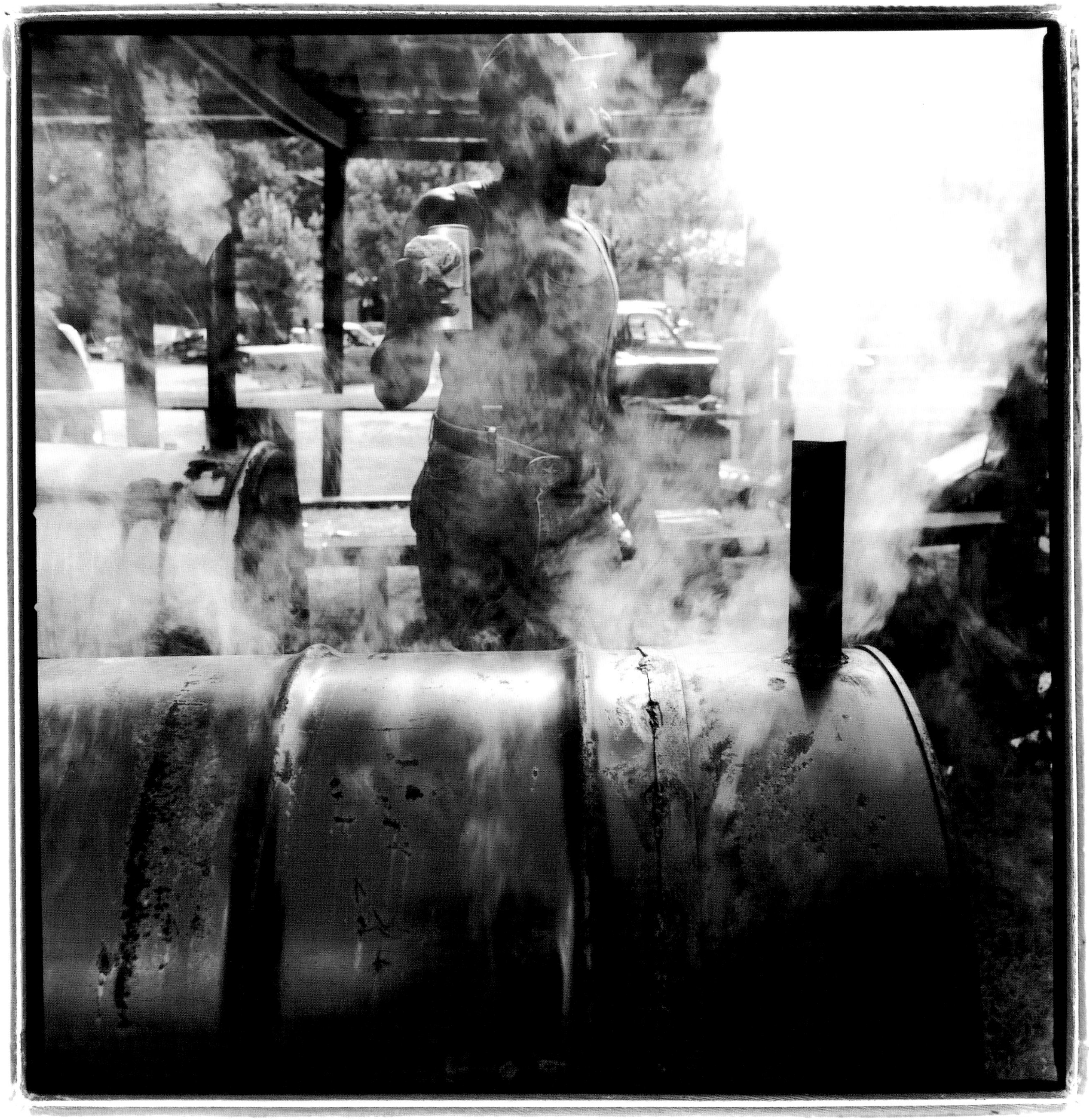

Smokers

Reunion Dance

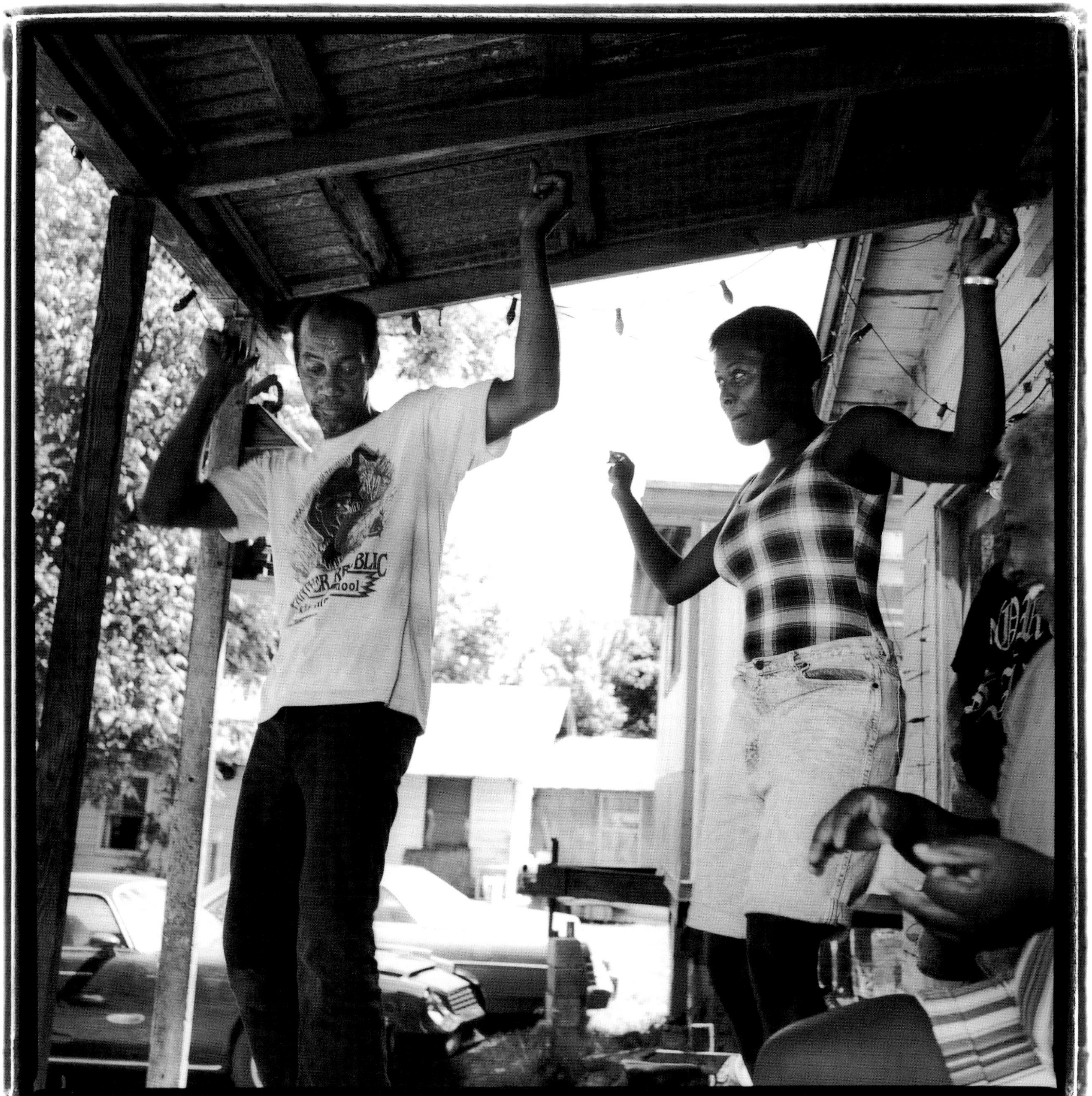

Rose

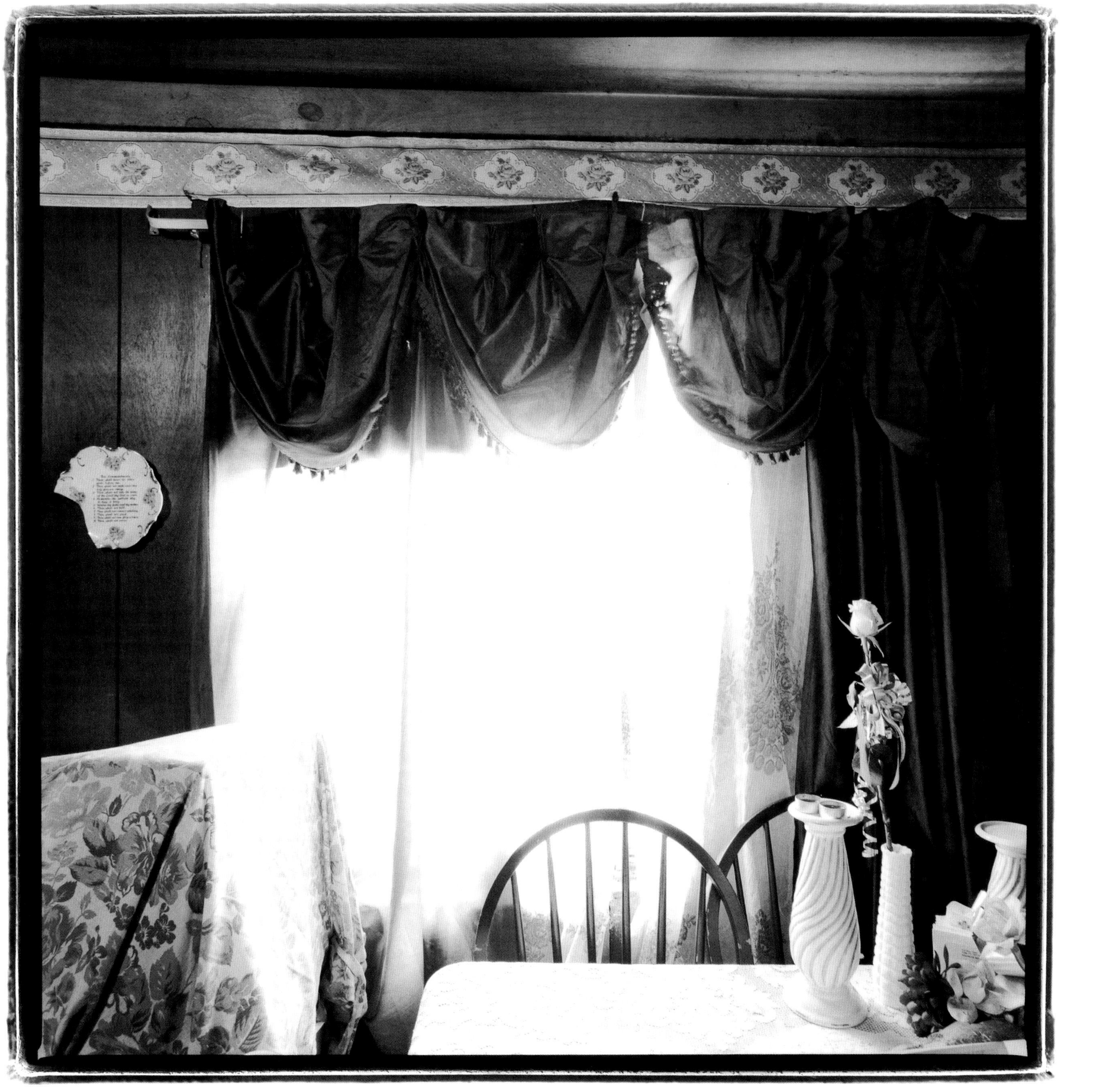

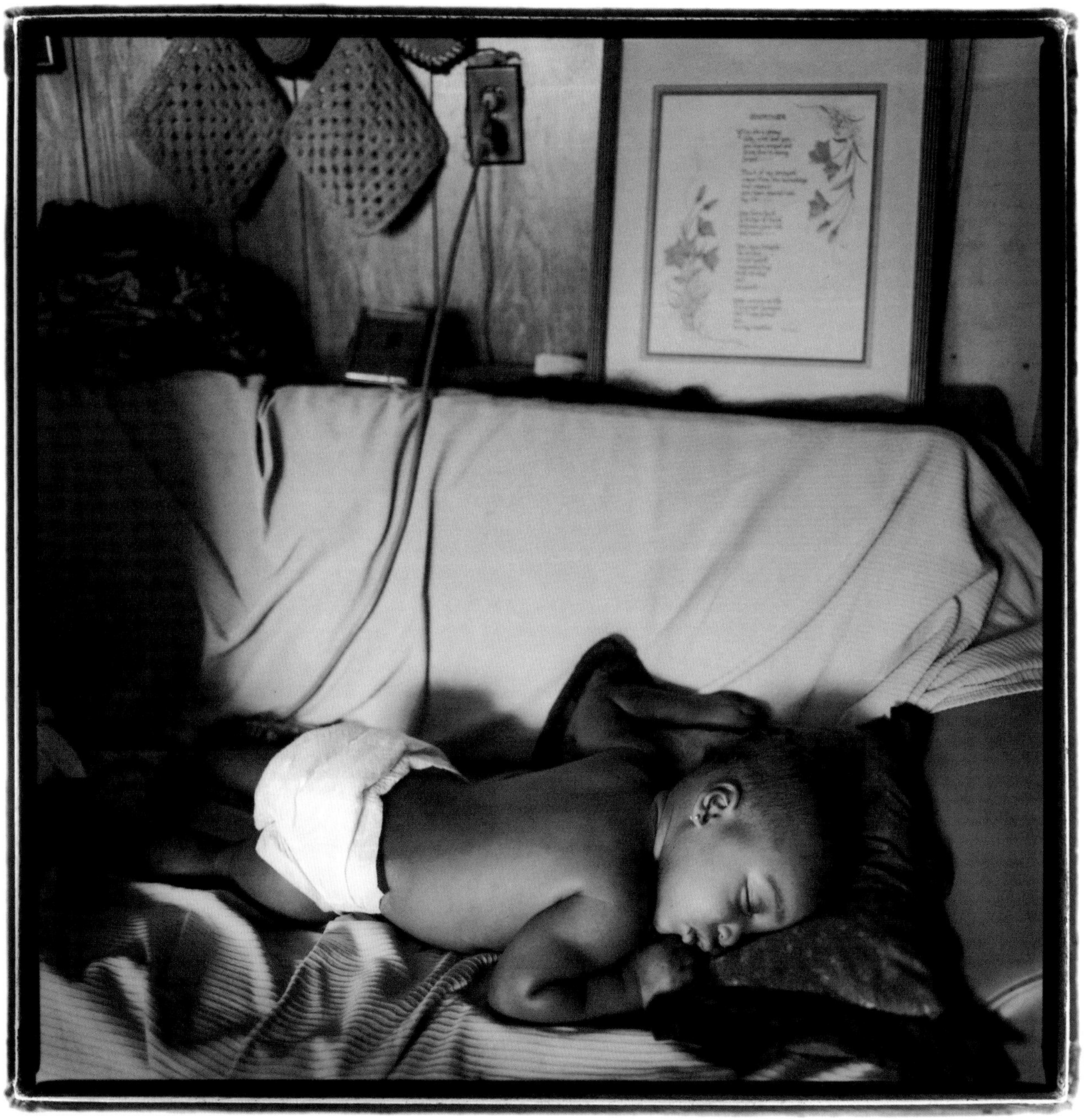

Asleep

Sleeping Baby

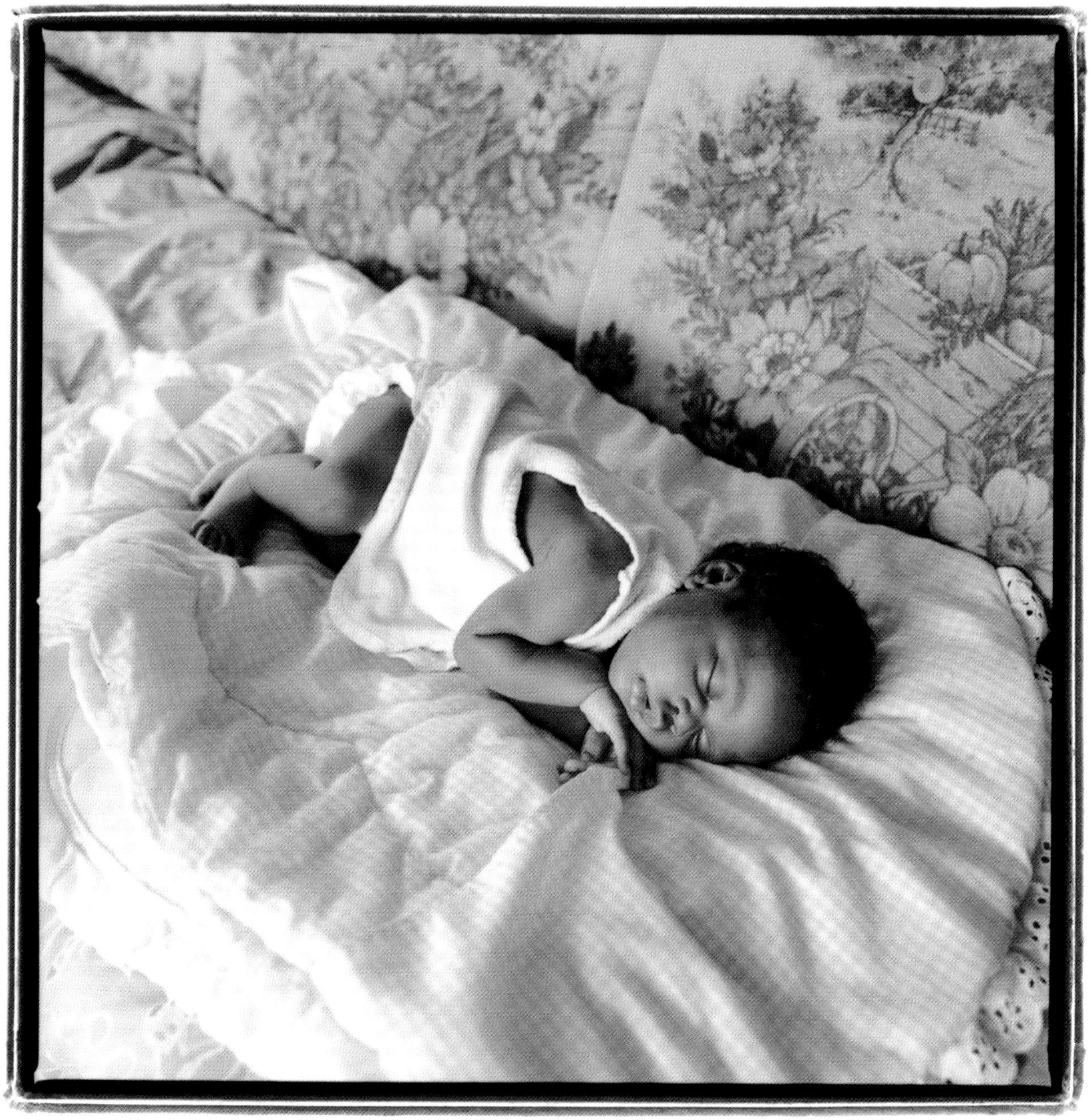

149

150

Reflection

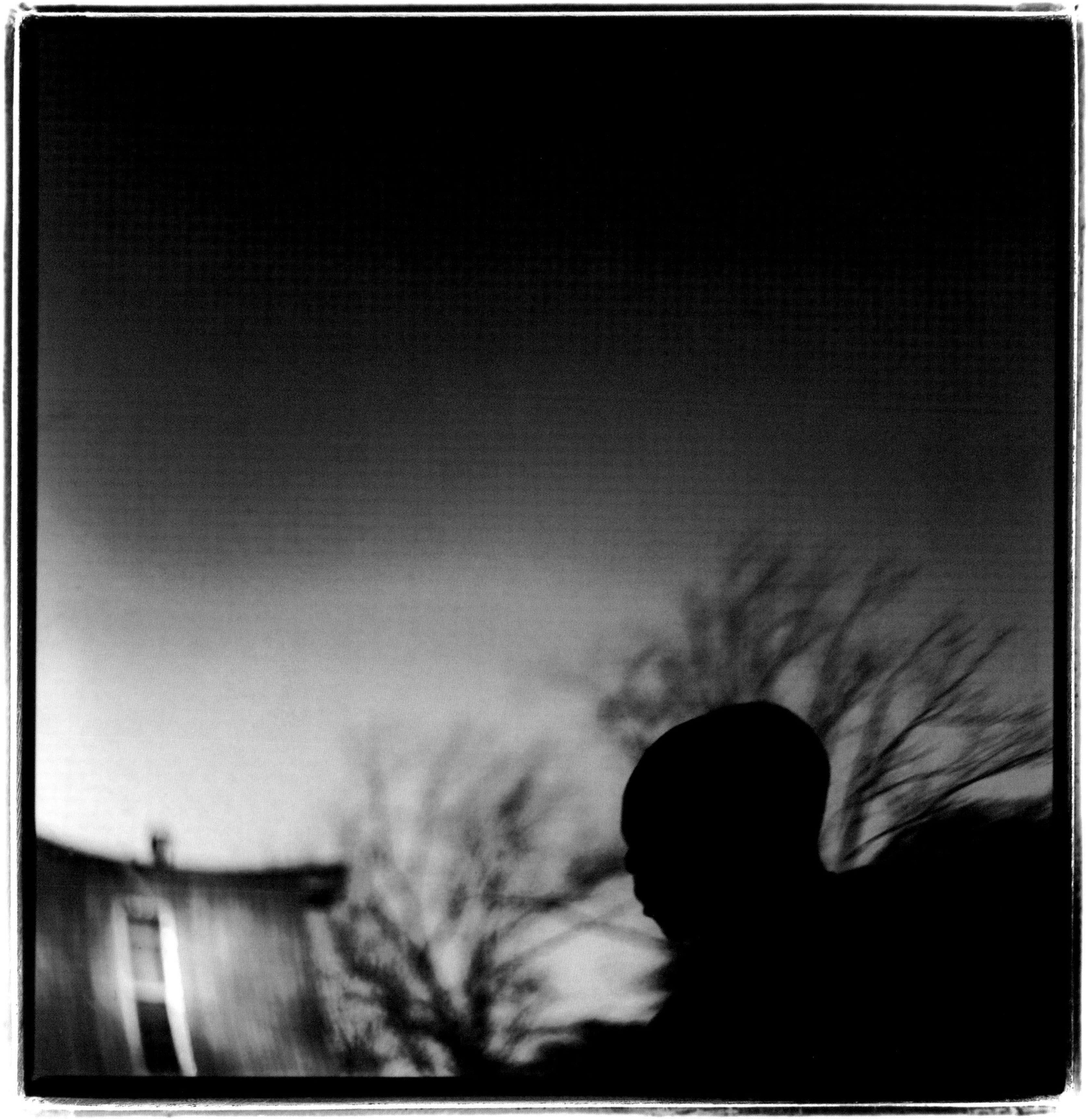

A Conversation *with* O. Rufus Lovett *by* Anne Wilkes Tucker

ANNE WILKES TUCKER: *When were you first aware of photography? What's your earliest memory of it?*

O. RUFUS LOVETT: My earliest memory was preschool, when I would go to my dad's darkroom with him and sit on a tall stool to peer into the sink as he processed prints.

So your dad was a photographer.

Yes, he was a teacher and the photographer at Jacksonville State University in Alabama. He met my mom there as a student, and after graduation he worked a while for a newspaper, then returned to Jacksonville State to teach media and do all the public relations photography. He minored in art, and I can remember him painting canvases when I was a child.

It's interesting that you would remember the darkroom and not him taking pictures.

Well, I remember that, too. But the darkroom was such a mysterious place as a small child. Those early years in my dad's darkroom are my first, fondest memories. This first memory of photography was when I was about four and five years old, too young to go on an assignment but not too young to sit and be awed by the darkroom.

Probably you were thoroughly photographed as a baby and as a child.

Pretty much, yeah.

And yet that interaction didn't interest you as much as watching the print come up in the developer?

That's right. I don't really remember the act of having a picture made of me, even when I look back at those studio and environmen tal portraits of me as a child. Growing up with a photographer, th camera experience seemed ordinary, and I was probably so used t a camera being around that it didn't leave a lasting impression o me as a baby. But the magic in the darkroom—that was special.

So your dad noticed your interest and encouraged you?

My interest in making photographs didn't come about until I wa in high school. My teachers asked me to become involved in th student publications.

That was Mrs. Horsfield?

Mrs. Dorothy Horsfield, the yearbook sponsor, and anothe teacher, Ms. Willie Mae Lee, who was responsible for the schoo newspaper. They knew that my dad would supply materials and th know-how to help me. I agreed to take on the work, and I enjoyed i

So when you picked up the camera, it was a 35 mm?

No, it was a 120 camera, a $2\frac{1}{4}$ x $2\frac{1}{4}$. My father didn't own a 35 mm camera in the early years. He had always worked with a medium or large-format camera. Other than a huge 5 x 7 studio portra camera, the first camera that I remember him using was a 4 x Crown Graphic. I remember loading the 4 x 5 film holders an carrying the gadget bags on my shoulders when he photographe events. I would go along to collect and discard the old use flashbulbs. Beginning in the early sixties he primarily used 120 camera.

So, even though you weren't taking pictures till you were in hig school, earlier you were assisting your dad?

Yes, when I was just a kid I would go along on his assignments an carry equipment and hold an auxiliary flash.

By osmosis you were picking up on decisions your dad made. Did yo learn to anticipate him in terms of . . .

Yes, and not only did I learn to anticipate what he expected me t do, but also I learned to anticipate what materials like film an ghting would produce. As a photojournalist, my dad had a formula nat he would follow in terms of exposure, lighting, and compo- ition. I remember his rapport with his subjects was wonderful. Ie has always used humor to relax and become acquainted with eople. Time was a factor and he worked fast. I still appreciate the bility he had to create so much in such a short amount of time nd achieve it with quality and consistency.

id you learn to bounce flash?

es, that and more in terms of lighting quality and direction. My ad was a great studio portrait photographer as well, and my expe- ience watching him in the studio continues to benefit my work.

nd different kinds of situational lighting?

n location assignments he would use a main flash near the camera nd usually insist on using an auxiliary flash, directional or ounced depending on the situation.

o you remember how your dad worked with people, how he instructed eople or didn't instruct people? Did he have a philosophy about that?

Ie was very structured and regimented in his photographic pro- edure because he dealt with timely publications that were short on pace due to advertising and copy demands. So he was careful about ne way he grouped elements and organized his photographs. He aught me a lot about cropping in the camera, and rarely did a pub- cation ever have to crop his photos. I have enjoyed this kind of ompositional control throughout my career. I continue to previsu- lize my compositions through the lens rather than at the enlarger.

id your dad work in photo essays, or were his assignments mainly ne-shot stories?

Ie mainly worked on one-shot stories, with an occasional essay. He njoyed the challenge of being able to tell a story with one picture.

id your dad do personal work? Did he have work that he did outside is job?

Iy dad took his job very personally, so I think the work he did for the university was his personal work. However, he did make environmental portraits, and explored the human condition and architectural studies on occasion.

Did your dad ever try to exhibit his work or publish it outside the university environment?

We have been in a couple of exhibits together since his retirement. However, before his retirement, other than his photographs being picked up by the Associated Press, there was very little time for exhibitions and other publications to be a consideration. He worked long, hard hours covering daily activities, evening events, weekend events, and athletic events. His time was totally con- sumed with the job at hand. He would do several shoots in the morning, process the film, force dry it, print it on fiber paper, force dry the print, and have it ready for the public relations department by noon. He would then repeat this procedure in the afternoon and oftentimes in the evening. That was routine for him for about thirty-eight years. I continue to admire all those photographers in the applied world whose work reflects their passion for photography. My father was one of those guys.

Did you learn from your dad the idea of deadlines and schedules?

Oh yeah, deadlines were a major issue, and I continue to stress that with my students. When I began assisting my dad and working with student publications, I became aware of deadlines on a personal level. But yes, definitely, a deadline was always an issue with my dad and being early to an assignment was an impulse my father lived. He is always early — an hour early — to anything that is going to happen, and I've become that way, too. Being early to photograph an event or a portrait subject on location helps me avoid missing something that might occur that is unexpected, and I find that it allows time for me to get in a "comfort zone" with an unfamiliar place.

Before we get on to your high school, you are starting to photograph, you have the influence of your dad, and your mom was a teacher; she taught literature.

Literature, English, composition, and a class on Robert Frost.

Are you a reader?

Not really.

So you didn't follow through with that family influence?

Not in terms of being an avid reader, but my mother taught me the importance of comprehending literature and the importance of communicating with words. One summer when I was home from college, I audited a creative writing class my mom was teaching. It was the first time that I had painted a picture with words rather than with light. I realize now how her class played a role in what I do, in terms of organizing thoughts for the visual literacy that I use in my photographs, even when I photograph in a more intuitive nonobjective manner. I will always value that experience in my mom's class. I went on to study journalism in college along with photography, but it was my sister who became the literary scholar and reader in the family. I've always been more involved in communicating visually.

You said in another interview that school was not your strong point.

That's right, I was a mediocre student at best in high school. It was not till I was well into college that I became consumed with learning.

So when you were given the opportunity to be a photographer you really . . .

Photography relieved the boredom that I experienced as a teenager in school; it really did. In high school I would even get permission to leave class to make a picture and I could have pretty much free rein to do that. It was a small-town atmosphere. Everybody knew my mom and dad; many of my teachers were taught by them in college because it was a laboratory high school connected with the university. Most of my teachers assumed that I was gifted like my sister [laughs]. She was valedictorian and made straight A's all the way through college. Teachers simply assumed that I was kind of like her. I wasn't, and got away with a lot in high school because of their erroneous assumption.

When you started photographing for the newspaper and the yearbook, when did you realize that what was "extracurricular" was what you wanted to major in? And did you choose a college accordingly?

It must have been around my junior—close to senior—year i high school when I was deciding where to go to college. Certain by my senior year, because my parents, as educators, were con cerned about that, of course; they didn't demand that I go t college; it was just kind of assumed that I would.

It seems to me that there are a couple of threads in your career that a pretty consistent. One is that photography was a part of your life fro the beginning. The other is that you grew up in a small town and yo chose colleges, undergraduate and graduate, in relatively sma towns; you now live in a relatively small town; and most of your phot essays have had to do with the life of a small town. It seems that thes early influences have remained dominant. I mean, you could hav chosen to study in New York or Chicago or lots of other places, but yo chose Sam Houston State.

Well, you have to understand that Sam Houston State was muc more affordable than some of those other places. We knew abou Brooks Institute in California and R.I.T. in New York, really fin photography schools, but it was more affordable and practical t go to a state college. It was already going to be pretty expensiv because I was going to have to leave the state and hence pay out of-state tuition.

Because there were no programs?

There were no photography programs in Alabama then, as a matte of fact. Sam Houston State was the only four-year photograph program in the South in 1970. Times have changed and now ther are many photography programs in an abundance of school Formal training in photography is not for everyone, but it worke out well for me. I wanted the credentials to teach on the colleg level. The best education for a photographer is to simply get ou there and do a lot of work, with experience being the key. Th college training may help speed up the learning process, and ma allow an opportunity for more information on a broader scope o subjects that may not get consideration otherwise.

One of your teachers there was John Beck?

John Beck was my most significant teacher. There were severa but he was the one who introduced me to fine art expressive pho

›graphy, and his demeanor as a teacher also played a major role ı my becoming a teacher.

'ere photographers such as Ansel Adams part of your awareness?

was aware, but not to any great depth at that time. John Beck ıtroduced me to the West Coast photographers and their expres-ive work. I had mostly centered myself in commercial portraiture nd photojournalistic work. I was even working on a double major ı photography and journalism. Later, my scope as a teacher and hotographer was broadened through the Ansel Adams workshops ıat I attended in the early eighties, once as a participant and nce when I was asked to return as an assistant. Adams and the eachers he brought to his workshops allowed an accumulation of nowledge unlike any other educational experience. I'll always emember that morning in Yosemite when Ansel Adams looked ıto my ground glass viewfinder and talked to me about previsu-lizing the composition.

'rowing up, did you look at Life *magazine and/or* National eographic, *or were there other magazines to which you found ourself gravitating?*

es, I looked at those kinds of consumer magazines but, at that me, I wasn't really seeing them critically in terms of what I ould do as a photographer.

'hen do you first remember becoming aware of the idea of a photo essay?

side from the work I experienced with my dad, I studied W. Eugene mith's photo essays, and John Beck would stress the importance f building a cohesive body of work. A photo essay is a body of 'ork, in my mind anyway, in which the individual pieces can tand alone, but when viewed together they interrelate, creating a articular point of view. I always compare, in the classes I teach ow, the photo essay with the picture story. The photo essay is a roup of photographs, with each image representing a paragraph nd several photographs developing a point of view. The photo ssay is composed of individual images that, when placed together, ecome interrelated. Each photograph in a picture story repre-ents a sentence, and several of them make a paragraph creating continuity and a story.

Without the sort of beginning and end—the narrative—that maybe a picture story would have?

Right, right, but maybe we are getting too academic?

I don't think that it's academic because these distinctions will be important when we talk about Weeping Mary *and the way you structured it. I am trying to lead to the way* Weeping Mary *evolved and how you conceived it. What photographers did you gravitate to when you began fine art photography?*

Certainly Ansel Adams, Edward Weston, Arnold Newman, and those who loved portraiture. I love photographing people. Henri Cartier-Bresson, Gordon Parks, Mary Ellen Mark, and Elliot Erwitt, who is one of my all-time favorites. Erwitt's wit is fantastic. I remember Arnold Newman once telling me that the most important thing I could do for my own photographic education would be to study art history. At that time I already had finished two degrees, but I went back to school to study art history, and traveled to Paris, France, on a self-appointed art history trip. Arnold Newman was right. I became much more aware of the language of art and its symbols and meanings, and how much art is a daily part of life.

Wit is something that you have continued. Some of your photographs are good for a chuckle. That is not necessarily where Weeping Mary *goes, but certainly some of the photographs you have published in* Texas Monthly *have an edge to them in that way.*

Sense of humor is an important aspect to just about everything, and I certainly try to use it in photographs and verbally to help establish rapport with my subjects, depending on the situation, of course. The situation dictates everything.

Have you always been easy with people? Has it always been easy for you to talk with people?

No, I was actually very shy when I was a child, and I think photography helped take some of that shyness away, starting with the work I did in high school. I was an introvert.

Because the biggest thread through your work is people. Even though you list Adams and Weston as influences, I don't think you are a traditional landscape photographer.

No, I'm not, but Adams and Weston influenced me as a craftsman and a thinker in terms of what to include and not include in a picture, the relevance of previsualization. John Beck introduced Ansel Adams's Zone System and the importance of finely executed prints. Perhaps at one point I became too anal-retentive about the craft. I will never forget George Krause looking at my portfolio of photographs made in Hong Kong and China. He suggested to me that I might loosen up a little bit [laughs], and I really appreciated that kind of criticism. I have relaxed in a way that has made me more aware of how chance can add to the improvement and understanding of a photograph.

When do you remember seeing a first print by a major photographer?

I was probably in school in the seventies.

Were there collections around, or did you see them in the city?

John Beck would have portfolio exhibits at the school. I remember early work by Ted Orland, and there were other images primarily from the West Coast.

He wanted students to see the quality of fine art prints, how they can be presented, and the language of presenting fine art work.

Yes, Beck related the importance of seeing original prints as we learn the craft of printing. So, I would visit the Cronin in Houston.

You would drive to Houston?

I didn't have a car [laughs], so I would hitchhike.

Then you graduated from Sam Houston and went to East Texas State. How did you choose East Texas State?

Teaching became a consideration as I finished my BA degree. John Beck suggested that I find a community college to begin a teaching career. To pursue a teaching career, the master's degree would be necessary. East Texas State University had just begun a photography program in the School of Journalism. Dr. Jack Bell, the department head, appointed me as a graduate assistant, and began an MA degree in journalism with a photography emphasis. I studied under Otha Spencer and Nolan Bailey. It was the perfec educational experience for me because it balanced my fine a background with John Beck and the commercial applied studie with Nolan Bailey. That kind of balance is crucial to the teachin I afford my students now at Kilgore College, because I teach fin art majors and commercial photography majors, allowing th various aspects from one area to complement the other. That' perhaps a rare notion in most schools.

It surprises me, both of your parents being teachers, that it was you college professor and not your parents that made you think abou going into teaching.

Well, it wasn't that my parents didn't make me think about teaching because I realized how successful they were in their teachin careers, but the fact that here was a new young mentor, who wasn my parents, and he made the teaching suggestion. That was significant influence for me. My folks have always been very ope and encouraging about whatever I wanted to do, and I'm sure the were pleased when I decided to become a teacher.

After you graduated from East Texas State, you got a job at Kilgor College in 1977.

After I completed my masters thesis, the job opening was there.

Kilgore is a community college?

Yes.

So you were going to a small college in a small town. Did tha feel comfortable?

I was pretty comfortable since I had always lived in a small-tow environment. It wasn't as comfortable for Frances, my wife because she's a city gal.

Yes, from Hong Kong to Kilgore is a big change.

Right. She had been living in Memphis, finishing a degree i

rchitectural technology at Memphis State University when we net. I was there for a year finishing up my graduate thesis. We got narried in Memphis and moved to Longview. The move to East 'exas was a pretty tough adjustment for her because Memphis sn't a huge city, but it is a city. Frances has adapted well and loves t here now. I'll always be appreciative of her sacrificing her nore-exciting metropolitan lifestyle for East Texas.

Iow big a town is Longview?

.ongview is about 70,000 . . . a little more, maybe. So it wasn't too ad in terms of size, but it was still quite an adjustment for her, nd at that time we didn't think that we would be here for more han three years, or at most maybe five. It's been twenty-eight ears now, going on twenty-nine.

)id you take naturally to teaching? Was teaching something you ealized that you were going to enjoy?

Ay mom missed a PTA meeting to give birth to me. I literally rew up on a university campus and even attended kindergarten at he University of Alabama as my mother completed her master's legree. As a child, the Jacksonville State University campus ecame my playground. So, looking back, it was almost as if I was orn to be a teacher. Getting back to John Beck's influence, he vas such a wonderful teacher and so open to his students and villing to share. He not only taught, but he also made pictures, and hat was an aspect that impressed me. I have had some photography instructors who just taught their classes and that was it. 'hey didn't really make photographs, and I thought, God, that's razy. How can you be passionate about something you teach if ou don't practice it?

'hat was your master's thesis project?

wrote and documented a biography on the career of a photogracher in Northeast Alabama, Leon Kennamer of Guntersville, labama. He was a portrait photographer who became known in ommercial circles for his innovative principles of subtractive ghting used for outdoor commercial portraiture. So it was very ommercial subject matter as opposed to fine art. I learned so nuch from him about light control and the subtleties of light.

What was your first major personal project after you got to Kilgore?

I was interested in almost the opposite of what I am doing now in terms of the environment. I was fascinated with the inner city, doing street photography.

Where?

I would hit the streets in Houston, return to Memphis, and then I began to travel to Asia, visiting Frances's family. I would take weeks and sometimes entire summers to experience Hong Kong, Beijing, Shanghai, and Bangkok. Living my entire life in small towns created a breaking point. The city was something I was unaccustomed to, and I became eager to experience their cultural differences, their circumstances.

Did you switch to 35 mm? What cameras were you using?

I was using both, but my true love is the square $2\frac{1}{4}$ x $2\frac{1}{4}$ format camera.

Is your 120 one where you look down into the camera or where you put the camera up to your eye?

I use an eye level finder with my 120. I find it more efficient to use, especially for spontaneous photographs.

Were you making black-and-white photographs?

Yes. I grew up with my dad's black-and-white photographs, black-and-white pictures in newspapers, and black-and-white television. The black-and-white medium gives me an impression of reality and truth, yet I realize it is a departure from reality since my eyes do see color. Because we see in color, black-and-white tends to lend a beautiful abstract concept to the image. Rarely do I think in terms of color when I'm holding a camera, unless it is required for a particular commercial assignment.

The nature of city work is a lot of walking, looking, and trying to engage with people, especially people who are kind of intent on going someplace. How did that evolve for you?

I would go to a neighborhood or city street where there was activity with a camera, one focal length lens, and perhaps a tripod, and walk or simply hang out on a corner until something would occur or a fascinating person would appear. Communication is the key when you're interested in the human condition. Approaching a possible subject, I often start a conversation with the simple, honest explanation that I'm photographing the street life in the area for an art project. Typical photographs would include people waiting for a bus, children playing, folks relaxing on the street or on their front porch, and even prostitutes and transsexuals.

Some street photographers pull back, use a wide angle lens, and capture a fairly large segment of the street. You tend to come right up to the people. You don't include a lot of environmental context. Is that conscious?

I often use a wide-angle lens, but rather than pull back, I move in close. I want to create a sense of intimacy with the people and subjects that I photograph. The wide-angle lens also allows me the capability to hand-hold at slower shutter speeds in low light levels without crippling the spontaneity. Although the people in my pictures are often the larger subject in the frame, the wide-angle lens also allows enough important environmental nuance to suggest a recognizable sense of place. I think that revealing the connection of people and place is important in most of my pictures, even if the environment is simply a plot of bare earth. It may, for instance, communicate a humble lifestyle significant to the character.

Was that your style in the city, or was the city different?

I see the early city street photographs, in Houston and Memphis particularly, as sort of a training ground for the work I'm doing now—not only in terms of visual communication but also in terms of learning to create an understanding between myself and my subjects. I am much more acquainted with my friends in Weeping Mary than I was with the street people. I have a much greater familiarity with Weeping Mary, partly because it's where I'm from, a small rural community. I find a closer relationship between me and the people I'm photographing more valuable now than with the earlier street pictures. An empathetic connection on some level is often a fundamental requisite for a successful photograph.

The first of your projects that I was aware of was the Kilgore Rangerettes. Was that your first picture published in Texas Monthly?

Yes, I began photographing the Kilgore College Rangerette during their fiftieth anniversary in 1989. In 1990 DJ Stou published a highkick image on "The State of the Art" page i *Texas Monthly*. Since then, I've been working with the magazin on a variety of editorial projects, and in September of 2004 *Texas Monthly* published a cover story on the Rangerettes tha included twenty-six images from my ongoing project from 198 to 2004. My magazine work is similar to my personal projects but usually more structured in a way that helps communicate th writer's, editor's, or art director's wishes. *Texas Monthly* certainl celebrates celebrity, but it also celebrates ordinary folks an their circumstances. I think the latter is where my work fits i the magazine.

So the Rangerettes are an ongoing project, if you will?

That's right, I'll be continuing the project this year.

Were any of the Rangerettes ever your students?

I have had a few Rangerettes as students, and some of the forme Rangerettes have become friends. I knew Gussie Nell Davis, th organization's founder and director, so I've had a long-tern relationship with the 'Rettes.

I ask that question because, looking at the Rangerette pictures, they ar less individuals as opposed to Weeping Mary. The Rangerettes are mor iconic. And that has a lot to do with their being in uniform, and a lot t do with the ritual of their performance; they are synchronized performers

My interest in the Rangerettes began with my attraction to th amusing contrast between the uniformed glamour and the foot ball turf, chain-link fences, metal bleachers, and asphalt envi ronments where they perform. The environment often plays a equal role in these photographs. Individual and close-up pic tures are part of the series, but the nature of this subject matte lends itself to a less personal interpretation of individuality; it' more about the circumstances and situations. Annie Leibovit once commented about the Rangerettes and how their individu ality doesn't seem to exist, as they have united to become one.

What year did you begin the Weeping Mary photographs?

t was the summer of 1994.

)escribe the drive to Weeping Mary. It's in East Texas, where you live, ut it's not that near.

ight. It's about ninety-five miles from where I live, between Nacogdoches and Crockett. The poetic name Weeping Mary was ike a magnet attracting me. I just had to go take a look.

After the turn at the Caddo Indian Mounds, the road curves nd winds down through a canopy of tall trees that leads to a iver-bottom flat. It's a road that gives me a sense of relaxation, a eeling that everything else behind doesn't matter anymore, that 'm here and that's all that matters. My first observation was a vooden bridge that crosses a creek, and then to the left stands a vhite wood frame church with a sign that reads, "The Church of Veeping Mary." I knew that I had arrived at a place that is very pecial. A little farther down, the road introduces a community of iomes and a couple of side streets leading to a few more homes naking up the neighborhood of Weeping Mary.

'ou weren't photographing?

No, I didn't take the camera out on the first few visits. That is one hing that I avoid doing at first glance. Even when I travel to Asia usually just go out for several days, without walking around with camera, simply to get over the excitement of being there. It ives me a chance to begin to see things, to just look and to get cquainted and comfortable with the people and the place.

eeing the church for the first time, what did that tell you?

t let me know that there is a settlement here, there is a community of families and it reflects a sense of unity. The first place I stopped o strike up a conversation was at Cherry Jenkins's place. Cherry was ery cordial as I introduced myself and later discussed the possibil-ty of making some photographs of the community. I discovered rom our brief conversation that everyone is interrelated in some vay: friends, cousins, uncles, aunts, parents, or grandparents.

o how many times a year would you go down to Weeping Mary?

'he first few years I would visit and photograph as often as possible. Summers allowed time to be there several times a month and sometimes two or three visits a week. My first visits were camera-less, as I mentioned. It was important to establish a rapport to avoid the intimidation that a camera is known to create.

So you just visited?

I paid visits in attempts to get to know the place and the people, and for me to become comfortable with the environment and also for people to be a little bit more comfortable with me. Anytime you're photographing a different culture, other than your own, even if it's within your own country, there's a sense of insecurity, on both sides, caused by the camera, probably. Certainly, considering the history of African Americans in this country, suspicion of my interest is understandable. Especially with the older folks in the community, who remember the lack of respect shown their predecessors due to the long and inexplicable existence of ignorance.

How would their suspicion manifest itself? What kind of questions would they ask?

"What are you taking pictures for? Why do you want to take pictures here?"

And what would you say?

My first response was that I'm a photography teacher making pictures for an art project. My friend who first told me about the place called Weeping Mary, editor and publisher Gary Borders, asked to publish a photo essay about the children of Weeping Mary in the Nacogdoches newspaper, the *Daily Sentinel*. This project gave me a credible reason for making the photographs and fulfilled my passion for photographing the people here. We did a couple of photo essays about the children of Weeping Mary and then later another, "Christmas at Weeping Mary." They were published in the *Daily Sentinel*.

Was it on your third visit to Weeping Mary that you started to photograph?

I think I began to photograph on about the third or fourth visit and made a couple of pictures. I remember one of my first pictures was of a grandmother cleaning fish while her grandkids hovered around.

So immediately, one of the first pictures you are describing not only has children in it, but it has generations. Looking at the body of work, those are two of the major themes that run throughout the project: children and generations. The interaction of generations has to be one of the things that fascinated you about Weeping Mary, because it is so prevalent. Is that right?

Yes, I think the photographs help illustrate growing up in Weeping Mary, and how the growing up there is intertwined with neighbors, siblings, cousins, aunts, uncles, parents, and grandparents. They all take care of and respect one another. My first impression and my last impression is this wonderful sense of unity and caring throughout the community.

Another dominant theme is community gatherings, whether they're reunions or holidays. When you were walking around talking to people and you heard about a reunion coming up, did you consciously put it in your book and try to be back?

Yes, early on I was invited to the family reunions. It seemed like hundreds of people from all around would attend these festive and spiritual reunions.

Did you make lists of things you wanted to photograph? Was there a desire to become comprehensive, or were there just certain things that you responded to that you decided to focus on?

I prefer going in without preconceived notions and just allowing events to occur. I enjoy the spontaneity and the possibility that chance and surprise can play a part. Mary Ellen Mark once stressed to me that photographers aren't observers, they're interpreters. I think that too much planning can get in the way of the unexpected events that may happen, and a unique interpretation may be lost.

Even though I don't do much picture planning before going there, that's not to say that I don't make specific decisions about a composition or ask someone to turn a face this way or that way or stand over here or position hands a particular way. That kind of control and planning becomes a part of my personal interpretation prior to making an exposure. So I do some directing from time to time, but not always.

While a large percentage of the photographs are outside, when di you first go inside?

I continue to mostly be interested in using the outdoors and out door light. I've made a few interior photographs in some of th homes, but I can't remember exactly when I first photographe inside. It must have just been a few years ago. It was perhaps 199 or 1998 before I photographed an interior.

Because that requires more trust?

More trust due to one's home being a much more private place tha the front porch or the front yard. I concentrate on the persona objects and treasures that accumulate over the years in a home.

Another theme might be objects that are precious to somebody, whethe it's a dress or even an egg or something that somebody is holding.

Trophies.

Yeah, the trophies in the window and in the living room. Is that anoth er way to convey something?

You know, that brings up a photographic issue. I photograph th human condition. It is a major photographic theme, so broad i scope, permitting other themes to help the visual literacy conve more about the humanity. The human condition theme may dea with portrait, landscape, still life, architecture, and even form an figure, all of which support my photographs of Weeping Mary. find it intriguing how our collectibles reflect so much about our selves: our families, pastimes, priorities, wishes, and ideals.

There's a quote that has been attributed to you: "I think the greatest most challenging, certainly most published photographs are those tha reflect the human condition." Is that the heart of what motivates yo in terms of photography?

Oh, absolutely. I think the more we study those around us in term of the way we live and our circumstances, the human condition the greater the contribution toward understanding one another Misunderstanding is a problem that most cultures appear t suffer from.

'hat would you most like someone who's looking at these pictures ɔ come away with?

'irst of all, it would be so easy for viewers of these images to et an incorrect surface impression that the pictures simply ocument an impoverished people and to feel sorry for the subects. In my mind this would be an incorrect and disrespectful onclusion about the place, the people portrayed, and the work tself. I would hope that those who see these photographs will ook more deeply and come away reveling in the celebration of caring humanity to which I have responded in these personal nterpretations. I remember when my sister, Opal, saw some of he early pieces of my work on Weeping Mary. As an artist, she oted that she sensed a feeling of dignity captured in the photographs. I think she is exactly right with her conclusion. And, or some of us, memories from days gone by will be sparked vhen seeing these pictures—as when you, Anne, remembered vhat a relative of yours might have said when you commented n the "Speckled Dog" picture. You remembered hearing them all out, "Git on, dawg."

Clothes hanging outdoors on a line may evoke fond memories f the smell of fresh laundry hung to dry. One art collector from Iouston, commenting on the photograph of the little boys riding he toy vehicle, said, "I can look at that photograph every day and t'll bring a smile to my face." And I would hope there will be hose who look at these images on an entirely different level ther than the literal specifics and discover a universality among s all. All of these ideas and reactions to the pictures sustain me nd my efforts with this project.

Veeping Mary is interesting too, because there are certainly elements f modern life.

'here are occasional nuances that relate to contemporary society, ut for the most part it's not really about that so much as it is bout the character of these people and the serenity that exists in his small rural community.

erenity is an interesting word, because there's nothing frenetic about hese pictures. They are people going about their life, but there is a ense of contemplation in the sitting and talking and interchange that s definitely not a part of city life. The other thing that is definitely not a part of city life is the animals. The ducks and slaughtering, etc.—that establishes it as rural. . . . Do you feel like you're finished with the project? It's been almost ten years.

This project started in 1994. I don't know when one is finished with a project like this. The children are getting older and I'd like to photograph them as they grow older. They're not as willing to be photographed as they were when they were little kids, so the challenge is greater in that sense.

But aren't there other little kids to take their place?

There are other children whom I haven't met, so there is that possibility and I might continue.

But is the sense of discovery waning for you? Was that part of the pleasure, the sense of discovery of this sort of intact place? Was there some element of curiosity for you?

The curiosity is not as great, as I have fulfilled my interest in certain aspects of the community. But, when I return to Weeping Mary now, there are other possibilities that I find exciting. I'm now more inclined to concentrate on the still life, and isolate elements within the community that approach a more abstract notion. A couple of the photographs that approach this abstract notion in this series are "Reflection" and "Earring." But, regardless of how much more photographic work I do at Weeping Mary, I will always know that there is a place filled with friends who have given me moments of their lives that I will cherish forever.

I think the thing that has impressed me about the work is that you genuinely admire Weeping Mary, you respect it, maybe even envy it a little bit. Most of us cannot go home again, but these people can and do, if they ever leave. There's something almost fairy-tale about Weeping Mary.

You are absolutely right about my admiration, and I do envy this place. That feeling you get, that there's something almost fairytale, goes beyond the fact that it is so isolated in a beautiful river-bottom flat. For me, there is a level of spirituality that I have never experienced anywhere else. It's difficult for me to explain in words. Hopefully, my pictures reflect these feelings best.

Acknowledgments The ten years this project has encompassed represent my passion for photography and countless days isolated from my family, whose understanding and unselfish encouragement are testaments of love. It was my wife, Frances, who first said, "Take your prints out of the box and show them to someone." • Throughout my career I have made numerous friends within the photographic community who have shown sincere support for my photographs of Weeping Mary. I wish to express my feelings of gratitude to a few of those friends, beginning with Roy Flukinger, one of the first to recognize and collect my work. Roy possesses the rare talent of waxing knowledgeably and eloquently about the significance of photographs and thereby validating a variety of photographic visions by any number of photographers. His commitment to photography is renowned, and greatly appreciated. • I thank Clint Willour for his undying devotion to Texas photographers and his uncanny capacity to recognize and present relevant new work. His talent has contributed so much to the photographic success of many. • Warmheartedly, I thank Jean Caslin, who first commented on the prolific nature of my Weeping Mary work and whose words of encouragement meant so much. • To DJ Stout I owe a debt of gratitude for his obsession with photography and his determination to publish my Weeping Mary photos and others in *Texas Monthly*. And many thanks to *Texas Monthly* for its continued celebration of photography. • I will always be grateful to my longtime friend Gary Borders, whose insight and observations gave genesis to this endeavor. • I have great admiration for all those who are involved in the making of photographs, and who also share their photographic experience to benefit others seeking to make photography their instrument and passion in life. I wish to recognize Dan Burkholder, Keith Carter, Michael Kenna, Mary Ellen Mark, and Bill Wittliff for their years of support and encouragement of this project and for the inspiration they have provided in the realm of photographic education. With great pleasure I also extend recognition to my former students, who have challenged me and inspired my growth as a teacher and photographer. • With special thanks I recognize a friend and colleague with whom I have worked for over twenty years, Bettye Craddock. She has served as a light of inspiration throughout my teaching career. • I express much appreciation to Bill Bishel and Dave Hamrick at the University of Texas Press for inviting the publication of these images and text. • With deep sincerity I acknowledge my dear friends Richard and Martha Rorschach for their kind generosity, as well as for their years of support of my photographic work and the photography program at Kilgore College. • I feel extremely honored to have Anne Wilkes Tucker's essay as an essential component of this book. Anne's insightful observations reflect a great understanding of my selected photographs and my approach to this body of work. She brings to this publication not only her photographic wisdom, but also her personal experiences as a southern girl who genuinely understands the culture that sustains the South. • Finally, I take this opportunity to pass along a warm thank-you to all my friends who are the residents of Weeping Mary. With your serene sense of humanity, you have shared with me moments of your lives that have made my life more fulfilled. O. Rufus Lovett